Peyton Randolph and
Revolutionary Virginia

Peyton Randolph (oil painting by John Wollaston between 1755 and 1758). Randolph was Speaker of the House of Burgesses, 1766–1775; Moderator of the 1st Virginia Convention, 1774; President of the 2nd and 3rd Virginia Conventions, 1775; President of the First Continental Congress, 1774; and President of the 2nd Continental Congress, May 1775 (Virginia Historical Society, No. 1858.6).

Peyton Randolph and Revolutionary Virginia

ROBERT M. RANDOLPH

McFarland & Company, Inc., Publishers
Jefferson, North Carolina

Library of Congress Cataloguing-in-Publication Data

Names: Randolph, Robert M., 1936– author.
Title: Peyton Randolph and Revolutionary Virginia / Robert M.
    Randolph.
Description: Jefferson, North Carolina : McFarland & Company, Inc.,
    Publishers, 2020 | Includes bibliographical references and index.
Identifiers: LCCN 2019044372 | ISBN 9781476679556 (paperback) ∞
    ISBN 9781476638621 (ebook)
Subjects: LCSH: Randolph, Peyton, 1721–1775. | Virginia—Politics
    and government—1775–1783. | Legislators—United States—
    Biography. | United States. Continental Congress—Biography. |
    United States—History—Revolution, 1775–1783—Biography.
Classification: LCC E302.6.R23 R36 2020 | DDC 975.5/02092 [B]—dc23
LC record available at https://lccn.loc.gov/2019044372

British Library cataloguing data are available

ISBN (print) 978-1-4766-7955-6
ISBN (ebook) 978-1-4766-3862-1

Front cover image: *Peyton Randolph*, John Wollaston, oil on canvas,
18th century (Virginia Historical Society, No. 1858.6).

Printed in the United States of America

McFarland & Company, Inc., Publishers
  Box 611, Jefferson, North Carolina 28640
    www.mcfarlandpub.com

To my father and mother, Nowlin Randolph
and Marjorie McGehee Randolph Head,
and dear friends over a lifetime,
with all of whom I have frequently sat up late
at night and discussed matters historical.
They have sharpened my analysis of, as well as
my interest in, historical issues.
This book concerns the choice presented to
many people in many ages, the dreadful choice
between war against apparently greater power
or submission. My friends may recall discussions
of these and similar topics. To attempt to list
such friends is to run the risk of a wedding invitation
list; viz., how could I have possibly left out ABC
and XYZ? Nevertheless, they are:
Charles Michael Matkin
William Martin Mount
Wallace Kuehn Tomlinson
Chase Stuart Wheatley, Jr.
Samuel Alexander Denny
J. T. (James Thomas) Walker
Richard G. Williams
Jonathan G. Kerr
George Parker Young
Ed L. Huddleston

Table of Contents

Table of Contents

Table of Contents

List of Illustrations

Acknowledgments

One of the features of this work has been the assemblage in a single book of copies of the portraits of all the leading actors in this drama and photographs of the originals or the reproduced locales in which these events took place. This has not been done before. One of the nicest features of doing so has been the number of helpful, pleasant people with whom I have dealt in assembling these illustrations.

First and foremost are the staff of the Colonial Williamsburg Foundation. In the first instance is Paul Aron, then chief of Publications, who took the time to read a sample of the draft, to meet with me and discuss it, to advise regarding potential publishers, to contact one of them for me, to vouch for the draft, and to put me in contact with the staff who could make copies of the Foundation's collection available. That person, in repeated periods over almost three years, is Ms. Marianne Martin in the Visual Resources Center of the John D. Rockefeller, Jr. Library. She repeatedly took the time to research her sources to advise me of the potential owners of portraits of the leaders during this period. She gave me the name of the owner of the portrait of Governor Fauquier, the Coram Children's Foundation in London, and, when they were unresponsive, she found that Bridgman Images had the portrait in their collection of available illustrations. On another occasion she put me in touch with the owners of a particular portrait, from whom I was then able to receive their permission. Over the course of almost three years she has been unfailingly helpful and pleasant, for which I am very grateful.

Dr. J. Kent McGaughey, Houston Community College, Northwest, published the primary biography of Richard Henry Lee, which had a copy of a color portrait of him on its cover. I had met Dr. McGaughey in Houston not long after his biography came out. I urged him to do a biography of Peyton Randolph, which he declined, and suggested that I do so instead. I suppose that was the initiation of my project. I contacted him again in 2016 to ask where he had found the color portrait of Lee, and he referred me to Ms. Judith S. Hynson, Director of Research & Library Collections at the duPont Library at Stratford Hall. I contacted Ms. Hynson, who took considerable time and effort to help me track down the color portrait. She was very pleasant to deal with, and I am appreciative of her efforts.

Richard Bland produced the pamphlet in 1766 which converted the Virginia minority who had been willing to concede Britain's right to tax the colonies. An early portrait of him has disappeared but Peter Frederick Rothermel obviously had seen it when he painted *Patrick Henry Addressing the House of Burgesses in the Stamp Act Debate.* Other figures shown in the painting can be identified as good representations of other men present, so it is reasonable to conclude that the representation of Bland is a good one. Richard Bland College of William & Mary is due credit both for spreading his name and fame today and also for having a portrait of Bland done, taken from the Rothermel painting. My thanks go to Ms. Irene M. Handy, the Richard Bland College librarian, who had a digital copy of this painting made for me, an effort far beyond just allowing me to copy an existing one.

I appreciate the assistance of the staff of the Washington & Lee University Collections of Art and History, particularly Ms. Bridget Pumm and Ms. Rebecca Williams. The portrait of Washington in his uniform as a Virginia militia colonel is the youngest portrait of him painted from life, and they were attentive and helpful in the permission for use of this portrait.

The Virginia Historical Society, along with the Colonial Williamsburg Foundation, is the other primary source of portraits covering the colonial and Revolutionary periods in Virginia. While there is some overlap of coverage, the two collections are generally different in coverage, and what one of them does not have, the other one probably will. They are the two principal sources of the illustrations in this book. As shown by the fairly numerous illustrations from other sources, neither collection is totally comprehensive, but the staffs of both collec-

Acknowledgments

tions are generally aware of the locations of other works and were helpful in pointing me in the right direction to look for them. At the Virginia Historical Society, Mr. Jamison Davis was particularly helpful in both regards.

The third large collection which assisted me is the National Portrait Gallery in Washington. Because it covers so much larger space in both area and time, it tends not to be so comprehensive for a particular period, but it does fill some of the holes in the more local collections. Mr. Erin Beasley, its digital image rights and reproduction specialist, was especially considerate not only in handling my requests for permissions of the portraits they had, but also in suggesting places to look for the ones I was missing.

In my reading I find that the First Continental Congress gets short shrift. The Second Congress has most of the action, including the Declaration of Independence. Yet the First Congress took the essential step of legitimizing in all the colonies the creation of parallel governments not subject to the royal control, a step which actually occurred and made further action possible. The Congress also legitimized non-importation policies in all colonies. It was not the fault of the Congress that non-importation was no longer effective, because it sought policies in Britain diametrically opposed to Britain's secret policy. The improved exposure of Carpenters' Hall to the general public may help remedy this situation. I have been assisted by the enthusiastic reception of this book by the staff of the Hall, especially Ms. Alicia Bono and Alex Palma, and their making illustrations of the Hall available.

Overseas, the staff of the Berkeley Castle Charitable Trust, especially Ms. Helen Berryman, its visitor business assistant, has been helpful in supplying the portrait of Sir William Berkeley. Likewise, the Scottish National Portrait Gallery, especially Ms. Dunant, has expedited our transaction and provided the portrait of Lord Dunmore.

I am especially grateful for the learned assistance of my consultants, Erica Jennings of Jennings Design and Judith Emmert in the Dallas area. I have found that much of what I was taught about grammatical usage in school and in university long ago does not accord with the best current practice, and they had the job of persuading me of that fact on more than one occasion. Their contributions to the fin-

Acknowledgments

ished product are manifold, and I have benefited greatly from their learned and friendly advice.

At the level of more intimate contacts, a number of family and friends have been kind enough to take the time to read the then-current draft of the manuscript and give me their ideas and/or encouragement. First and foremost of these in their impact on the shape of the manuscript is my beloved daughter, Jeanette Randolph Rollins ("Jeanie"), the best-educated member of our family, who has done occasional work as a professional editor. Jeanie read it in its original chronological, plodding form. She picked up on the fact that the British policies were connected with the ultimate goal of enriching favored politicians in Britain by milking the colonies—"like a large Ireland"—and insisted that this intent should not be buried in a chronology but rather highlighted from the start. All of which was immediately apparent, once she pointed it out.

Lyn Tomlinson of New Orleans, who has done public relations work in many forms, a friend of the family for fifty years, read the manuscript. She asked permission to give it to a friend of hers in New Orleans, Michele Gallman, a retired teacher from Austin who has also done editorial work. The two of them made a number of suggestions, particularly relating to style, many of which appear in the manuscript, for which I am very appreciative.

Two of my former partners and long-time friends, Jon Kerr and George Young, both of a historical bent, read the manuscript and encouraged me to proceed further with it. Their encouragement regarding the usefulness of this work in filling one or more holes was uplifting for me, especially when I experienced the common problems of an author looking for a publisher.

Finally, I am grateful to my beloved wife, Stephanie Wyn Randolph, for her loving patience while I spent many hours working on this project, which could otherwise have been spent profitably looking after her and our own affairs.

Preface

I attended my first year of college at the University of Virginia. While in Virginia, I was surrounded by reminders that the American Revolution *was not* the beginning of America's story but rather *was* the culminating event of a society that was more than 160 years old. Despite the radical consequences of the decision to take on militarily the most powerful empire in the world, it also appeared that the colony of Virginia had gone into revolution almost without a dissenting voice.

As years went by, I became aware that contrary to the simplified story taught in high school and college history books, the American Revolution was not uniformly approved in all the colonies. Worse yet, I learned that in most colonies, the war against the British Empire also involved civil war within the colony.

The most loyal and most desperate opponents of revolution eventually sought refuge in places like Boston, New York, and Charleston, and more than 80,000 Tories emigrated as the tide of empire ran out. South Carolina endured a particularly bloody civil war. North Carolina fought a strange, localized war against Tories whose fathers had been driven from Scotland by King George II, grandfather of the current king, King George III. Philadelphia was full of Tories. New Jersey's governor, the Tory son of Benjamin Franklin, was supported by many. New York, fearfully divided, was the only colony that may have had a Tory majority. Connecticut had to put down its Tories by armed force. Massachusetts had Tories by the thousands. Tories who surfaced when the British took Georgia in 1778 had to be evacuated from Savannah with the British army in 1782.[1] In all these colonies, many leading men supported the Crown. Only in Virginia, and there alone among the major colonies, did the colony go into revolution united. The Tory men of consequence there literally could be counted on a single hand. The merchants were mostly foreign (Scots) agents of Glasgow firms and were hated long before they sided with the Crown.

Many years ago, I began to wonder how it came about that only Virginia went out united. The more I read, the more apparent it was that the Virginians, while deeply divided as to the remedy for their grievances, were more united regarding their rights than any other colony.

As I read further, it became apparent to me that the critical difference between Virginia and other colonies was the difference in leadership. More precisely, the difference was made, as so often in history, by a single man (Churchill comes to mind).

This work argues that the man was Peyton Randolph.

I accept the description of one historian that "historians have described a small, able ruling group, largely members of the planter class and frequently related by family ties. These men governed both through the Council and to an even larger extent through the House of Burgesses, and their dominance of the County Courts and the Anglican parish vestries provided additional bases of local power. A further concentration in the hands of a few leading Burgesses meant that a dozen or so men might dominate the government of the colony. At the same time a relatively wide franchise for the election of Burgesses prevented the ruling elite from ignoring the will of the populace and suggested a wide assent to the government of the colony."[2]

Clifford Dowdey claims, "It produced more great men in government than any other society in a comparable period and a comparable space."[3]

How did Virginia go into the Revolution united, when no other major colony did so?

Forty years and more after the events that occurred when he was a college student or a young man, Thomas Jefferson wrote in a letter to William Wirt: "We slackened our pace, that our less ardent colleagues might keep up with us, and they, on their part, differing nothing from us in principle, quickened their gait somewhat ... and thus consolidated the phalanx which breasted the power of Britain. By this harmony of the bold with the cautious, we advanced with our constituents in undivided mass, and with fewer examples of separation than, perhaps, existed in any other part of the Union."[4] Jefferson identified the "less ardent colleagues" as Edmund Pendleton, George Wythe, Richard Bland, Peyton Randolph, and Robert Carter Nicholas and the "bold" leaders as Patrick Henry, the Lees, the Pages, George Mason, Jefferson, and others.[5]

While other major issues existed, as shown below, the fundamental issue in Virginia was the constitutional issue. From the Stamp Act of 1765 through 1775, Virginia reacted almost as strongly to actions against other colonies as it did to actions against itself.

We shall see that almost every leader in Virginia believed that Britain had violated the constitutional rights of Virginia. (By the "constitutional rights of Virginia," the Virginians understood those rights to be the rights of all Englishmen under the English constitution, as modified and enlarged by statutes and precedents applicable particularly to Virginia.) They differed as to the means of redress. Jefferson's description of the process by which Virginia achieved unity when other colonies' divisions became intractable was self-serving. The radicals did not willingly "slacken their pace." How were the radicals restrained from proceeding too rapidly and aggressively, splitting Virginia as other colonies were split? If Peyton Randolph did it, what did he do?

1

Painting with a Broad Brush[1]

In 1763, the Treaty of Paris ended the first world-wide war, known in America as the French and Indian War and in Europe as the Seven Years' War. The war had started in Virginia, and Virginia contributed greatly to it. The Virginians looked forward to prosperity: access to the lands beyond the Appalachians granted to Virginia more than 150 years previously and repeatedly confirmed to them, access at last to the Indian trade in the Ohio Valley, and access to the Continent for their tobacco, their primary cash crop.

Powerful men in London planned otherwise. Soon after agreement on the Treaty of Paris in 1763, the Board of Trade (also called the Lords of Trade), who oversaw the day-to-day policies over all the North American colonies, adopted and submitted a proposed new policy to the Privy Council, the committee at the apex of the pyramid of executive power and closest to the King. King George III personally approved the change of policy, and it was announced and known as the Proclamation of 1763.

All land west of the Appalachians was reserved for the Indians. New land grants and new purchases from the Indians were prohibited. Upon inquiry by the Governor of Virginia, the Board of Trade ruled that all prior grants of land across the mountains were void, defeating many prior grants, great and small. Settlers who had already crossed the mountains were ordered to return. Licenses to trade with the Indians were required to be obtained from the royally appointed Superintendents of Indian Affairs. The Superintendent for lands north of the Ohio River issued licenses to Philadelphia merchants, who had the exclusive right to operate out of Fort Pitt (Pittsburgh) for their enrichment and that of their friends in London.

1. Painting with a Broad Brush

Word was put out in London that the purpose of the Proclamation was to pacify the most serious Indian war in almost a century.

The real purpose was recited in a communication from the Board of Trade to the Privy Council, when Western land policy was again being debated in London in 1772. "We take leave to remind your Lordships of that principle, which was adopted by the Board, and approved and confirmed by His Majesty, immediately after the Treaty of Paris, viz.: the confining the western extent of settlement to such a distance from the sea coast, *as that those settlements should lie within the reach of the trade and commerce of this kingdom, upon which the strength and riches of it depend, and also of the exercise of the authority and jurisdiction which was conceived to be necessary for the preservation of the colonies in due subordinance to, and dependence upon the mother country"* (emphasis supplied).

This policy was never publicized or admitted at the time, but its existence was gradually surmised by different colonial leaders at different stages of the events. A Tory Ministry moved several Acts through Parliament pursuant to this policy in 1764. The Stamp Act was prepared beginning in 1764 and enacted in 1765, but all as part of the same secret policy. It was signed by the King in March 1765. After its enactment by Parliament, the Secretary to the Treasurer (the Prime Minister) wrote, "The great measure of the session is the American Stamp Act; I give it the appellation of *a great measure* [sic] on account of the important point it establishes, *the right of Parliament to lay an internal tax upon the colonies"* (emphasis supplied).

Opposition to the Stamp Act in the colonies, effected by cessation of trade with Britain, so alarmed the British merchants as to bring about a change to a Whig Ministry and the repeal of the Stamp Act in March 1766.

With a respite of barely a year, a new Tory Ministry returned to its old policy. A series of Townshend Acts were enacted, one of which, in June 1767, taxed paper, lead, paint, glass, and tea sold in the colonies. This was clearly an internal tax, but it was largely hidden by being imposed on the merchants rather than on the consumers. Resistance to the Act was slow in forming. The tax on so few articles would raise only a small fraction of the cost of administering and defending the colonies, the purported reason for the tax. But Townshend openly told the House of Commons that he "would 'in time' do everything to form a *revenue to bear the whole, but by degrees and with great delicacy"* (emphasis supplied).

A Pennsylvania lawyer, John Dickinson, aroused the colonists' opposition with a series of twelve letters from "A Farmer" published that winter, which were reprinted in twenty of the twenty-six newspapers in the colonies. He pointed out that Parliament increasingly had prohibited the colonies from buying from nations other than Britain and from selling to nations other than Britain. It had also prohibited manufacturing in the colonies that might compete with British manufacturers. If Parliament could tax the goods that could be imported only from Britain, the colonists could be milked and turned into "abject slaves."

The tenth Letter exhibited Ireland as an object lesson, following imposition of permanent taxes in Ireland. *"Besides the burdens of PENSIONS in Ireland, almost all the OFFICES in that poor kingdom have been bestowed upon strangers.... In the same manner shall we unquestionably be treated, as soon as the late taxes levied upon us shall make posts in the 'government' and the 'administration of justice' HERE worth the attention of people of influence in GREAT BRITAIN"* (emphasis in original shown as capitals, and other emphasis supplied). Dickinson showed how the cost of pensions and offices had been increased by £158,000 in only two recent years.

At that time, there was only one sinecure that burdened the taxpayers of Virginia. The Burgesses appropriated the money to pay the Governor, appointed by the Crown. The Governor, a well-connected politician or courtier in Britain, collected a £6,000 annual salary and hired a Lieutenant Governor to go to Virginia and do his job for 50 percent of the Governor's salary. Dickinson had painted an alarming picture of what the future held, as experienced by Ireland.

Virginia was the oldest colony, and its history differed from the others. Its legislature had exercised the exclusive right to levy internal taxes for 140 years, and the efforts of parliaments and ministries to do so were overwhelmingly considered to be unconstitutional. A pamphlet published by a Virginia lawyer during the Stamp Tax controversy laid

1. Painting with a Broad Brush

out the historical, constitutional claims of Virginia and resulted in virtual unanimity in Virginians' conviction of their rights far beyond the degree of internal agreement in any other colony.

Virginia's unity carried it through the Revolutionary War. The Peace Treaty of 1783 provided for compensation for Tory emigrants whose property had been confiscated. In Virginia, only twenty-four claims were filed by native-born Virginians. In radical Massachusetts, with a white population the size of Virginia's, 203 native-born Massachusettsans filed claims, 8.5 times the rate in Virginia.

Virginia was almost evenly divided as to the means of redress up to the last minute before the Revolution, but—unlike the other colonies—the leaders came together and the "less ardent" participated in the leadership of the Revolution and of the Commonwealth. They were not driven into the political wilderness or even into exile, as was the norm elsewhere.

Time after time, the margin of votes that moved Virginia toward revolution could be measured as fewer than the fingers on one hand. Who was able to count the votes in advance and, tailoring the proposal to attract enough votes to pass, then persuade the essential handful to take the next step toward revolution? At every critical juncture, we find the presence of Peyton Randolph. I submit that it was he who allowed, and often led, the movement into revolution. The "radicals"— Patrick Henry, Richard Henry Lee, Thomas Jefferson, and even George Washington—were constrained to take small steps forward without losing contact with the larger mass who gradually came to believe that Britain did indeed intend to subjugate Virginia as if it were another Ireland, a cow to be milked.

In an even more deeply divided body, the First Continental Congress, Peyton Randolph as its President, moved it toward revolution with even narrower margins.

Jefferson described Peyton Randolph in his *Biographical Sketches of Distinguished Men.* He was "loved and respected by his friends," certainly not unusual. He was "somewhat cool and coy toward strangers, but of the sweetest affability when ripened into acquaintance. Of Attic pleasantry in conversation, always good humored and conciliatory." He was "learned in the law and highly regarded, but indolent in business which caused him to get less business than otherwise." He was not eloquent, but commanded more attention, which "gave him weight in the House of Burgesses which few ever attained."[2] While Jefferson acknowledges the unusual "weight" that Randolph had in the Burgesses, nothing in his *Sketch* of Randolph indicates why he had such "weight."

During the First Continental Congress, dour Silas Deane of Connecticut wrote his wife: "Our President [of the Congress] seems designed by nature for the business. Of an affable, open and majestic deportment, large in size, though not out of proportion, he commands respect and esteem by his very aspect, independent of the high character he sustains."[3]

We are dealing with an extraordinary politician. He wrote no pamphlets and made no stirring orations, though he occasionally spoke in debate. He was a man who was at his best in company, who carefully observed those around him and practiced politics as persuasion, an art of the possible. His real work was done in small, informal gatherings.

While he participated in the writing of reports, to and of the public's business, but invariably had others do the drafting, his personal correspondence is nonexistent. He disclosed the reason in his response to Landon Carter, a kinsman, his wife's uncle, who complained of receiving no response to a succession of letters: "I must own, I don't like the business of writing, not from idleness neither, but because I had rather read the productions of any man's brain than those of my own. Your threatened adieu has made me set down to write a letter about nothing."[4]

Consequently, we have very little testimony from Randolph's own mouth or pen as to what his thoughts and intentions were. He moved slowly and cautiously toward independence. There was a major movement in his position between 1765 and 1769, as we shall see, but then a steady movement away from Britain. Was his movement reactive to British aggressions, being pushed away involuntarily? Or was it a considered movement toward an end—independence—that he privately foresaw no way to avoid?

Because of his public activities, he was better informed of events

1. Painting with a Broad Brush

in Britain and in other colonies than any other man in Virginia. I will describe in detail the actions of which he had information and that would have affected his analysis of the situation in which Virginia found itself. Most histories of the period do not describe in chronological sequence the major aggressions of Britain against the colonies due to the need to abbreviate the length of the work or to emphasize the subject matter of the book. But here, we are trying to examine the working of a man's mind, which he himself did not disclose, except insofar as he deemed it necessary and prudent to do so. Since Randolph was the best-informed man in Virginia regarding matters affecting his colony, his "country," I will set these out in greater detail than one usually finds.

It is the thesis of this work that Randolph foresaw the drift of Britain's policy and the likely result flowing from it at a fairly early date—December 1768 through April 1769—and that it was his work to hold Virginia together as it went into the storm. His success enabled Virginia to lead the new nation for almost fifty years.

(Since this work sometimes also refers to Peyton Randolph's father, brother, and a multitude of other Randolph relatives, where any of them are involved, I will refer to Peyton Randolph and to his kinsmen by their full names in order to distinguish him from them. Otherwise, I will refer to him simply as "Randolph," and the shortened reference will be exclusively to him.)

2

Peyton Randolph's Family and Early Career

Peyton Randolph was born in Virginia on September 10, 1721. He was the son of John Randolph and Susannah Beverley Randolph. They had four children: Peyton, John, Beverley, and Mary.

Peyton Randolph's father, John Randolph, read law in London at Gray's Inn and was called to the Bar in 1717. He returned to Williamsburg and soon married Susannah Beverley. He returned to London to represent the College of William and Mary in 1728 and the General Assembly (composed of the Council of State as an upper house and the House of Burgesses as the lower house) in 1732. He was knighted in 1732—perhaps the only man born in the North American colonies, and certainly the only man born in Virginia, to be so honored. Sir John became Clerk of the House of Burgesses and, after resigning to be elected the member for Williamsburg, was elected Speaker of the House of Burgesses and then, concurrently, its Treasurer. He died young in 1735.

Peyton Randolph's mother, Susannah Beverley, was a daughter of Peter Beverley, the Clerk of the Burgesses in 1691–1692. Her mother was a daughter of Sir Edward Peyton, Baronet. Susannah and Sir John Randolph gave their first son his grandmother's maiden name, which is how the name Peyton entered the Randolph line.[1] Another of their sons was given his mother's maiden name, Beverley. This practice was already established in the family. One of Sir John's brothers had been given their mother's maiden name, Isham.

See the appendix for earlier family history, including how and why the Randolphs came to Virginia and how they became close to Governor Sir William Berkeley, to their great benefit.

2. Peyton Randolph's Family and Early Career

Sir John Randolph, 1955 copy in oil on fabric by John W. Guenther of a 19th century painting by Edward Caledon Bruce, itself a copy of an 18th century miniature (Virginia Historical Society, No. 1956.15).

Lady Susanna Beverley Randolph, 1955 copy in oil on fabric by John W. Guenther of a 19th century painting by Edward Caledon Bruce, itself a copy of an 18th century miniature (Virginia Historical Society, No. 1956.16).

Peyton Randolph was educated at the College of William and Mary. He entered the Middle Temple in 1739 and was called to the Bar as a barrister (a trial lawyer) in 1742. He returned to Williamsburg and soon married Elizabeth (Betty) Harrison. She was a daughter of Colonel Benjamin Harrison and Anne Carter Harrison of Berkeley. Her brother was also a Benjamin Harrison, the fifth of that name, a lifelong friend of Peyton Randolph's and a signer of the Declaration of Independence. Betty's maternal grandfather was Robert "King" Carter, the richest man in Virginia in his day, who successfully endowed each of his children. Peyton and Betty Randolph, however, were childless.[2]

Peyton Randolph practiced law in the colony's capital, Williamsburg. Governor Sir William Gooch appointed him Attorney General in 1748. In October 1748, Williamsburg elected him its Burgess. In the 1752–1755 House, Peyton Randolph served on three of the five standing committees and was chairman of the Committee on Courts.[3]

The French and Indian War began in 1754 with Virginia's creation of a militia regiment, commanded by Colonel George Washington, promoted after the death of its first Colonel. Governor Dinwiddie sent the regiment to occupy the forks of the Ohio River and build a fort there, now the site of Pittsburgh. The French had arrived there first and built their own Fort Duquesne. After the defeat of this expedition, Randolph recruited 150 cavalry, equipped by themselves, to aid in the colony's defense. Randolph was commander of this unit, which saw no combat.[4]

Randolph was promoted to chairman of the Committee on Elections and Privileges, the second most important committee. In the 1762 session, he became chairman of the Committee on Propositions and Grievances, the senior committee. As its chairman, he was also chairman of the House when it sat as a Committee of the Whole.[5]

Elizabeth Harrison (Betty) Randolph, John Wollaston, 18th century, oil on canvas painting (Virginia Historical Society, No. 1927.19).

In 1752, Governor Robert Dinwiddie sought to impose a fee for his signature on all land grants. The Burgesses sent Randolph to London as their representative to oppose what they regarded as an unconstitutional tax. Governor Dinwiddie removed Randolph as his Attorney General for accepting a commission inconsistent with his representation of the Governor. The Board of Trade in London side-stepped the constitutional issue by disapproving the fee and ordering Governor Dinwiddie to reinstate Randolph as Attorney General.

3

Speculation in Western Lands

In colonial Virginia, the ways to create wealth were to raise tobacco profitably, to trade with the Indians, and to speculate in Western lands. The latter involved receiving land on or beyond the frontier by grant, by financing the passage of new immigrants ("headrights"), or by purchase. The land was then held for its increase in value by advancement of the frontier and its ultimate resale to planters replacing land exhausted by tobacco culture, to "new men," to small planters and farmers, or to intermediate speculators who would continue to hold it.

It should be no surprise that the politics of Virginia, and of other colonies also, were more complicated than the textbook history of heroic revolutionaries against evil Tories. Because Virginia had much more extensive claims to Western lands than any other colony, land speculation was a major factor in its internal politics.

The Crown grant of land to the Virginia Company in 1612 extended to the west and northwest from sea to sea. The Board of Trade in London set the price and terms of sale of public lands. The General Assembly, with consent of the Governor, could make special grants, usually politically motivated, but subject to approval of the Board of Trade.

In 1744, Governor Gooch appointed Thomas Lee, the builder of Stratford Hall, as Virginia's representative to a council held at Lancaster, Pennsylvania, between Virginia, Pennsylvania (represented by James Patton of Pennsylvania), and the Iroquois. The Treaty of Lancaster confirmed the 1612 grant to Virginia. In 1745, John Robinson, Speaker of the Burgesses and Treasurer of Virginia, and others organized the Greenbrier Company, soon renamed the Loyal Company, to

14

petition for a grant along the Greenbrier River, now in West Virginia along its Virginia border, south of the Ohio River. The company's shareholders were primarily Robinson's supporters between the James and York Rivers ("the Peninsula"), Randolph among them, and some new men with interests on the Piedmont frontier, including Edmund Pendleton and Peter Jefferson, who was the husband of Randolph's first cousin, Jane, the daughter of Isham Randolph, and father of Thomas Jefferson. Isham Randolph was the builder of Tuckahoe in Henrico County above the Falls. The Burgesses and Council, with the approval of Governor Gooch, granted 100,000 acres to the Loyal Company. They granted 100,000 acres to James Patton, who had been Pennsylvania's representative at the Lancaster Council. They also granted John Blair, Sr.'s Blair, Russell & Co. 100,000 acres on the Potomac and Youghiogheny Rivers, south of the forks of the Ohio. None of these companies had any obligation to build forts, trading posts, or even settlements. These companies sought simply to turn land at a profit.[1]

Lee thereupon petitioned the Governor on behalf of a group mainly from the Northern Neck (the peninsula between the Potomac and Rappahannock Rivers and Chesapeake Bay), for Governor Gooch's support of a grant of 500,000 acres north of the Ohio River. The grant would be conditioned upon the building of forts and trading posts in order to strengthen the British position against the French. Governor Gooch declined to support Lee and his friends.[2]

Thomas Lee appealed Gooch's refusal of the petition to the Board of Trade. In 1748, the Board of Trade overruled Governor Gooch and approved Thomas Lee's petition. As modified by the Board of Trade, an initial grant of 200,000 acres north of the Ohio River was approved. The grant was conditioned on settling 100 families in the grant and building a fort and trading post. That would earn a second grant of 300,000 acres north of the Ohio, likewise conditioned on settling another 200 families and building another fort and trading post. The Board of Trade's approval reflected the structuring of the plan to advance imperial interests by protecting the claimed area against the French and opening new markets for British merchants among Indians and new immigrants. In 1747, Lee organized the Ohio Company to perform the terms of the grant. He patterned the company on the original Virginia Company, creating a sound base in London. The English shareholders included Members of Parliament and leading London merchants with interests in the Indian trade or Virginia. By 1752, the Virginia shareholders included Northern Neck interests such as Lawrence Washington, half-brother to George, George Mason, John Taylor of Caroline, Richard Henry Lee, Thomas Ludwell Lee, Francis Lightfoot (Frank) Lee, Philip Ludwell Lee, John Mercer, John Tayloe of Mount Airy, and Tidewater men, notably Robert Carter of Nomini Hall, and Governor Robert Dinwiddie. Mason served as its Secretary from 1749 until his death. His uncle, John Mercer, served as Treasurer. Thomas Lee's son, Arthur, was appointed the Ohio Company's agent in London.[3]

In 1749, a 400,000-acre grant on New River in Southwestern Virginia was made to a group of 18 men, including Randolph, Edmund Pendleton, and John Madison, father of James Madison. This grant was unopposed by the Northern Neck interests. In October 1751, a month before the arrival of the new Governor, the Council extended the grant to Blair, Russell & Co., which had expired in 1749. John Blair, Sr., was a leading member of this Tidewater group.

In 1751, Governor Robert Dinwiddie arrived in Virginia. He was a professional imperial administrator who agreed with the goals of the Ohio Company, which would further imperial interests in the West by closing the Ohio River Valley to the French in Canada.[4] He became a shareholder in the Ohio Company. In 1752, he convened a conference at Logstown, down river from the forks of the Ohio, between Virginia, the Western tribes, and the Iroquois. It confirmed the Treaty of Lancaster and also allowed the Ohio Company to make grants south of the Ohio River, potentially in conflict with the Loyal Company. Within a year, the Ohio Company began settling families on the frontier, having built a storehouse in 1749 on the upper Potomac and done preliminary surveying in 1750. Speaker Robinson, Peter Jefferson (surveyor for the Loyal Company), Edmund Pendleton, presumably Randolph, and others opposed the Ohio Company as interfering with their own scheme. John Blair, Sr., asserted the overlap of his extended grant with the Ohio Company's. This brought on a critical delay in the operations of the Ohio Company and probably prevented its timely completion of a fort at the forks of the Ohio. Pennsylvania speculators also opposed the Ohio Company. Although the 30,000,000-acre grant to William Penn did not even begin to approach the Ohio River and Valley, Philadelphia traders had gone into the Ohio Valley long before the Ohio Company began entering the Ohio Valley trade.[5]

In 1753, information was received in Virginia of French plans to encroach on the Ohio River Valley. Dinwiddie sent George Washington, a young Ohio Company surveyor, to take a message to the French on the upper Allegheny River, demanding that they stay out of the Ohio River Valley. The French sent him back to Dinwiddie with the message that he should address their Governor in Quebec City. In 1754, Dinwiddie authorized Washington to recruit a militia unit to build a road to the forks of the Ohio and build a fort. A few miles short of the site of Pittsburgh at the forks of the Ohio, Washington found that the French had seized the Ohio Company's partially built fort at the site and completed it as Fort Duquesne. He was forced to withdraw and, after a skirmish at Fort Necessity, he and his men surrendered.[6] Following this defeat, Randolph organized a force of 150 cavalry, self-equipped, to assist Washington in defending the frontier. They saw no combat and disbanded before the arrival of General Edward Braddock.[7] Dinwiddie notified the Board of Trade that if the French were not expelled, the English trade with the Western tribes would be lost.[8] While Dinwiddie and the Board of Trade viewed this conflict through the imperial lens, Robinson and the Loyal Company viewed it as primarily between themselves and the Ohio Company. Dinwiddie's support in the Assembly was chiefly the Northern Neck interests, which, as we have seen, were a minority in the Burgesses but had support in London.

In 1755, Philip Lee (executor of the estate of his father, Thomas Lee) and Augustine Washington (father of Lawrence and George) were elected Burgesses from Westmoreland County. Philip began distributing the estate to his brothers: land in Stafford County to Thomas Ludwell Lee and land in Loudon County to Frank Lee. In 1757, Dinwiddie appointed Philip to the Council. His brother, Richard Henry Lee, and his cousin, Richard "Squire" Lee, were elected for Westmoreland County, Thomas Ludwell Lee for Stafford, Frank Lee for Loudon, and cousin Henry Lee for Prince William. The Lees and their friends, such as Robert Carter, were a powerful bloc in the Burgesses.[9]

In 1755, General Braddock was sent to Virginia with a large body of regular troops. George Washington was Colonel on General Braddock's staff in the advance over Washington's wilderness road toward the French Fort Duquesne. Not far from their destination, Braddock was ambushed and killed. The retreat of the regulars was organized by Washington and covered by Virginia's militia. This defeat opened the entire Virginia frontier, including the settlers recently settled by the Ohio Company as part of its contract, to the horrors of Indian war. The colony finally united against this threat. Francis Fauquier succeeded Governor Dinwiddie in 1758. He found the Robinson faction, dwelling mainly in the proximity of his capital at Williamsburg, to be congenial, and the Northern Neck faction lived far away.

In November 1758, the French abandoned Fort Duquesne. British officers and a Pennsylvania delegation concluded a treaty at Easton, Pennsylvania, in October 1758 with the Iroquois and some Western tribes in which Pennsylvania agreed not to establish settlements west of the Alleghenies without the Indians' consent. Under pressure of the British commander, Governor Fauquier acceded to this treaty, undercutting the Ohio Company and Virginia's claims to the territory.[10] The following year, the Philadelphia merchants did £30,000 of trade with the Indians out of the new Fort Pitt at the Forks of the Ohio.[11]

After the war was over, the Ohio Company was financially incapacitated by its losses on the frontier at the beginning of the war and by litigation between one of its principals, Philip Lee, and a key London merchant. Therefore, in 1763, a new company was formed—the Mississippi Company—by all the Lee brothers except Philip and by George Washington and others to secure a 2,500,000-acre grant directly from Parliament, with 50,000 acres allotted to each of fifty shareholders. It would be obligated to settle 200 families within the watersheds of the Ohio, Wabash, and Tennessee Rivers, avoiding the Loyal Company and Blair grants. A portion of the stock was reserved for Members of Parliament. Arthur Lee was their agent in London.[12] This plan was aborted by the Crown's Proclamation of 1763, discussed herein below.

4

The Attorney-General
Chooses Between Loyalties

It is difficult to look into a man's mind when he leaves little mark of his words and thoughts except in his official documents. Nevertheless, when a man's course of action conforms consistently to a principle throughout his lifetime, we may reasonably conclude that we know his mind in that regard. Peyton Randolph's conduct during the Pistole Fee controversy is the first time we can know with certainty where his primary loyalty lay.

Governor Robert Dinwiddie arrived in Williamsburg in November 1751. As was the case with most "Governors" of Virginia, he legally was the Lieutenant Governor. A politician or courtier in Britain closer to the government than Dinwiddie was the nominal Governor, who hired a Lieutenant Governor to do his work. The normal division of the Governor's salary, paid by the taxpayers of Virginia from the colony's revenues, was half to the Governor and half to the Lieutenant Governor. Dinwiddie, however, had agreed to a split giving him only 40 percent of a £6,000 annual salary, planning to make up the difference, plus a profit, through other perquisites of his office.

Patents conveying land by the Crown to the first grantee from the Crown were issued over the signature of the Governor. When Dinwiddie arrived, 1,700 patents awaited signature in his office. The Burgesses convened, did their business, and went into recess. Dinwiddie still had not signed any patents. After the Burgesses left town, Dinwiddie took advice from an unusually weak Council, who approved his proposal, and then announced that he was initiating a fee for signing each patent, which went to him personally for discharging one of the functions of

19

his office. The fee was one Pistole, a Spanish coin equal in value to five-sixths
of a pound (£), 16 shillings, 8 pence
(16/8d), more than triple the cost
of purchasing 100 acres from the
Crown, five shillings (5/-).[1]

The Burgesses were furi-
ous. They regarded the fee as
an internal tax, which constitutionally required the Burgesses'
approval. At the next session of
the Burgesses in spring 1753, the
House resolved that the Pistole
Fee was "illegal and arbitrary." A
committee, composed of Richard
Bland, Charles Carter, and Carter Burwell, was created to write a letter to Dinwiddie. Bland had
assembled the largest collection of legal works and records
pertaining to Virginia in the colony and was generally regarded

Governor Robert Dinwiddie, C(harles?)
Dixon, Great Britain, miniature watercolor
on ivory, probably 1749–1751 (Colonial
Williamsburg Foundation, No. TC1990-
0077. Gift of Sir Campbell Stuart).

as the leading constitutional lawyer in Virginia. Bland drafted the
House's letter. It argued that the Burgesses had the right to inquire
into grievances of the people, who may not be deprived of their property without their consent. Furthermore, the fee was contrary to precedent set by the Privy Council in 1689, disallowing an earlier Governor's
attempt to charge a similar fee. Dinwiddie responded that the Pistole
Fee was compensation for his labor in conveying Crown land, rather
than a tax, and refused to back off.[2]

The Burgesses next convened in October 1753. The House
appointed a committee to draft a petition to the King, consisting of
Bland, Charles Carter, Randolph (Bland's first cousin), Benjamin Harrison (Randolph's brother-in-law), Edmund Pendleton, and Joshua Fry,
Surveyor for Albemarle County (Charlottesville). The petition, drafted
primarily by Bland, was adopted by the Burgesses.[3]

The Burgesses also elected Randolph as their agent to present their petition and voted him an allowance of £2,500 (more than Dinwiddie's salary). Dinwiddie refused to approve the appropriation. After Randolph embarked for England, Dinwiddie also dismissed him as Attorney General and stopped his salary.[4]

Randolph presented the petition to the King. It was referred to the Board of Trade. After many months, the Board of Trade effectively ruled against Dinwiddie but dodged the constitutional issue. The Board allowed the fee in principle but denied its application to the 1,700 patents prepared prior to Dinwiddie's arrival, to patents of 100 acres or less and to patents for land west of the mountains (the larger grants). The Board denied Dinwiddie's effort to collect quit rents for the Crown between the date that a survey for patent was filed and the time a patent was issued. The Board also strongly recommended that Dinwiddie reappoint Randolph as Attorney General. When the Burgesses next convened in October 1754, Dinwiddie did so and also finally approved the Burgesses' grant for Randolph's expenses.[5]

For the purposes of this study, the primary significance of the Pistole Fee controversy was the conflict of interest in which it placed Randolph and his resolution of that conflict. His appointment as Attorney General for the colony was made by Governor Gooch in 1748 and continued by Governor Dinwiddie. The office of Attorney General was an office of the executive authority of the colony, an appointment by the Governor, acting on behalf of the Crown. His position required him to advise and represent the Governor, not the Burgesses, as well as to represent the Crown in the General Court, the highest court in the colony, in law, equity, and criminal cases. It was not believed that Randolph's position as Attorney General conflicted with his service as Burgess for Williamsburg, commencing in 1748 after his appointment by Gooch as Attorney General that same year.

As Attorney General, Randolph held the highest Crown appointment in Virginia, preceded only by the Governor. As a Burgess during the period 1751–1754, he was not a leading figure. He served on three of the five standing committees and was chairman of the Committee on Courts, the junior of the five committees. He was not on the special committee that initially engaged Dinwiddie, though he was on the

4. The Attorney-General Chooses Between Loyalties

enlarged special committee that drafted the petition to the King. On both of these special committees, the leading member was its chairman, Richard Bland.

Randolph likely was elected as agent for the Burgesses not because he held an official legal position as Attorney General, but because he was on any person's list of the half-dozen best legal minds in Virginia. Also, both he and his younger brother John Randolph had received their legal education in England, been admitted to the Bar, and undoubtedly had a wide acquaintance there. Furthermore, his father, Sir John Randolph, had also received his legal education and been admitted to the Bar there. Sir John had returned to England representing the College the first time and the Assembly the next for extended periods of time and was knighted in 1732. We may assume that Peyton Randolph had maintained or could revive some of his connections, though Sir John had been dead for eighteen years when Peyton Randolph returned to England in 1753. The English connections of Peyton Randolph and his family were important to him professionally as well as personally and emotionally.

It might have been possible for Randolph to have served on the second special committee in October 1753, because his role was minor. However, when he accepted election as agent for the Burgesses for the specific purpose of contesting Dinwiddie's imposition of the Pistole Fee, an action financially important to the Governor personally, there could have been no doubt in Randolph's mind that Governor Dinwiddie would remove him as Attorney General, thereby losing a significant income, and, in all likelihood, that there would be no chance of his again holding that office, perhaps ever, since he had chosen the Burgesses over the Crown, but certainly not so long as Dinwiddie was Governor. At the time Randolph made his decision, there was no way he could have known that Dinwiddie would be compelled to reappoint him.

These are the principle elements of the conflict of interest with which Randolph was faced in October 1753. As Attorney General, he held the next highest Crown appointment in Virginia and, if he discharged it to Dinwiddie's satisfaction, there was every reason to anticipate that he could retain that position for the duration of his career.

In addition to his ability, he had the finest legal education available and extensive family connections at the highest levels in Virginia. As a Burgess, he was rising in its ruling circles, the Tidewater group around Speaker John Robinson, but he certainly was not in a position of high leadership. Occupying the position he did, his choice would be widely noticed. By accepting his election as agent, Randolph unequivocally chose his loyalty to the Burgesses and to Virginia over his loyalty to the Crown and to England.

This was the paramount issue before Randolph. His unequivocal choice foreshadows all that followed. As the issues later arose that forced Virginians into conflict with Britain, he undoubtedly hoped to be able to reconcile their differences. At some point, after he had come to have more and better sources of information than any other man in Virginia, he concluded that the issues were irreconcilable. When faced with that conclusion, his choice of loyalties continued to be the one he had made in 1753.

It is odd that not a single one of the writers listed in the bibliography has noted or commented on the significance of Randolph's choice of loyalties at the time of the Pistole Fee controversy, at a high present price and most probably a high future price. Most—nearly all— of the writers follow Jefferson in calling Randolph one of his "less ardent colleagues," and most writers group him as a "conservative," holding back the "radicals." A former partner and dear friend of mine has commented that I "read a file differently" from other lawyers, and that is certainly true in this case.

The First Committee of Correspondence

By 1753, Virginia had a permanent agent in London who received his instructions from the Governor, though he was paid by the Burgesses. One undoubted effect of the strained relations between Governor Dinwiddie and the Assembly was the appointment in 1759 of a separate agent representing the General Assembly, rather than the colony or the Governor. A Committee of Correspondence was created to communicate with the agent and to instruct him. It was composed of four Councilors and eight Burgesses. An Act of the Assembly named

the members in 1759: for the Council, William Nelson, Thomas Nelson, Jr., Philip Grymes (husband of Peyton Randolph's sister, Mary), and Peter Randolph; and for the Burgesses, John Robinson, Peyton Randolph, Charles Carter, Richard Bland, Landon Carter, Benjamin Waller, George Wythe, and Robert Carter Nicholas.[6] Most of the members of the committee lived in or

Top left: Landon Carter, oil on canvas (Wellford Family / Colonial Williamsburg Foundation). *Top right: George Wythe,* William H. Crossman, 1927 oil on canvas, from 1791 John Trumbull sketch from life for Declaration of Independence painting (Colonial Williamsburg Foundation, No. KC13c. Gift of the Vestry of Bruton Parish Church). *Bottom: Robert Carter Nicholas,* silhouette (Virginia Historical Society, No. 2008.1.27).

near Williamsburg, so that the committee or a quorum thereof could be assembled on short notice. Randolph lived in Williamsburg rather than on any of his landed properties, and his renovated house can be seen in Williamsburg today. Randolph served on this Committee of Correspondence from then on. He became one of the inner circle who had access to the flow of information between Williamsburg and London and was thereby kept abreast of events in Britain affecting Virginia that surpassed the knowledge of virtually all other Virginians continuously from 1759 onward. His access to such information—"intelligence," if one prefers—commencing as early as 1759, in the course of time gave him an unparalleled knowledge of the events of his time in Virginia, the other colonies, and in Britain, insofar as they

General Court, Capitol, Williamsburg (Colonial Williamsburg Foundation, No. T1983-154).

affected Virginia. His future actions must be assessed in the light of that fact.

The Leading Lawyers of Virginia

During the period we have now entered, 1755–1775, the leading lawyers in the colony were Peyton Randolph, his brother John Randolph, Robert Carter Nicholas, Edmund Pendleton, George Wythe, and Richard Bland.[7] Pendleton and Wythe argued more cases before the General Court than the other four. An indicator of the widespread opinion as to who were the leading lawyers was the 1765 appointment by the Assembly of Peyton Randolph, John Randolph, Robert Carter Nicholas, and George Wythe to collate and publish the colony's laws, known as the Code of 1769. Each was paid £100 for his labors.[8] Pendleton was more a great trial lawyer and a master of debate in appellate work than a scholar, so it was appropriate that, of the leading lawyers, he was not on the list of those to do such scholarly work.

As one of the leading lawyers in the colony, Randolph had another source of information, namely the courthouse events and gossip that lawyers pick up. In his case, it was the gossip of the highest court in the colony in the capital of the colony. It was unlikely that anything of consequence occurred in Virginia during these years that Randolph did not know about.

5

Britain's Post-War Policy Toward the Colonies

With the approval of the Ministry in London, the "French and Indian War" began in Virginia in 1754 with the expedition of the Virginia militia, led by Colonel Washington, to occupy and build a fort at the forks of the Ohio River (modern Pittsburgh). Their defeat was followed by an expeditionary force of British regulars under General Edward Braddock, supported by Virginia militia, ending in Braddock's defeat and death in 1755. This was followed by the horrors of an Indian war on the frontier. These actions brought on the only world war to start in the Western Hemisphere, beginning in 1756. Known in Europe as the Seven Years' War, it raged across five continents, ending in 1763 with the Treaty of Paris, which ratified Britain's overwhelming victory and its newly won place as the most powerful Empire in the world. In North America, France lost Canada and Spain lost East and West Florida to Britain; Spain gained Louisiana as compensation from France. Britain, for the first time, controlled all of North America east of the Mississippi, except New Orleans.

In 1754, Governor Dinwiddie and the Council pledged a grant of 200,000 acres to volunteers for the expedition to secure the forks of the Ohio, of which 100,000 acres were to be in the area of Fort Pitt and the other 100,000 acres further south along the Ohio.[1] To finance the war, Virginia became the last colony to issue paper money, starting in 1755. In 1757, the new paper money was backed up by new taxes: a poll tax, an ad valorem tax on land, new license fees, and taxes on both imports and exports. It could be used to pay obligations to the colony at face value. As it was thus redeemed by the colony, the paper was to be retired and burned by the Treasurer. In 1757, the General Assembly provided that sterling debt could be paid in paper at a 25 percent discount. In 1759, the Board of Trade urged that all debts before 1757 still be payable in sterling, but the Burgesses refused to amend their Act. During the course of the war, Virginia issued £540,000 in paper currency to finance it. At one point, Virginia's war expenses were double those of all other colonies combined.[2] After Braddock's defeat, the British regulars moved north, with rare exceptions, and Virginia was left to defend itself for years.

With victory and expulsion of France on the horizon, the Virginians looked forward to peace and expansion on the frontier by removal of the French support for the Indians and to prosperity from the end of the war's disruption of the tobacco trade. Instead, they experienced a gradual unfolding of Britain's new imperial policy, the purposes of which were not publicly acknowledged. Differences in the pace at which different men reluctantly came to acknowledge the existence of the new policy largely explain the different reactions of Virginia's leaders.

The Proclamation of 1763

On October 7, 1763, King George III issued a Proclamation defining the new boundaries for each of the North American colonies, including the new colonies of Quebec, East Florida, and West Florida. All land west and north of the sources of all rivers flowing into the Atlantic was reserved for the Indians, though considered held by the Crown under military rule, together with all lands east of that line to which Indian title had not been previously relinquished. The Proclamation Line was declared effective "for the present, and until our further pleasure be known." It prohibited new land grants and new purchases from Indian tribes within this area and required licenses for all Indian traders. Settlers already living within the area were ordered to withdraw.[3] On inquiry from Governor Fauquier, the Board of Trade ruled that all preexisting agreements and grants were void, defeating large grants to both the Ohio Company and the Loyal Company, as well as reneging on the pledge of grants to Virginia's veterans.

The Virginians never questioned the Crown's right to control land grants.

It was widely believed at the time, even by those most affected, that the Proclamation was in response to Pontiac's War. This was the most serious Indian uprising since 1675, provoked by the high-handed treatment of the Indians by the British officers, led by General Jeffrey Amherst. They had acted in the belief that the defeat of the Indians' French allies now allowed the British to change the rules of frontier trade to the Indians' detriment. Thirteen British frontier forts were lost, beginning in March 1763, and hundreds of settlers and soldiers were slaughtered, mostly in the Great Lakes region. Even the Greenbrier River settlements in Virginia were attacked. Most Virginians viewed the Proclamation as a violation of the pledge of Western lands to its veterans and the rights of those already settled and the owners of large grants (including the Loyal and Ohio Companies).[4]

After settlement of the Stamp Tax dispute in 1766, the Proclamation Line was modified. In March 1768, the Board of Trade issued a report in which it stated that the Proclamation Line of 1763 was temporary. On October 17, 1768, in the Treaty of Hard Labour, the Cherokees ceded title to the area from Wytheville to the junction of the Great Kanawha and Ohio Rivers (southwestern Virginia and most of present West Virginia). The effect of this was confirmed by the Crown after the Ministry's decision to seek accommodation on the Townshend Acts in 1769. On November 7, 1769, at the opening of the General Assembly, Governor Botetourt advised that the King approved a further extension of this boundary with the Cherokees, provided that Virginia paid the costs of the negotiation.[5]

In March 1768, the Assembly advised settlers west of the Proclamation Line to avoid hostilities with the Indians rather than withdrawing.[6] In October 1768, Sir William Johnson, Superintendent of Northern Indian Affairs, met at Fort Stanwyx, now in upstate New York, with 2,200 Iroquois and other Indians, to clarify borders between Indians and colonists. The Iroquois ceded the area from Lake Oneida in upstate New York to Fort Pitt and everything south of the Ohio River to its junction with the Tennessee River in far western Kentucky.[7] These two treaties effectively breached the Proclamation Line. Nevertheless, when the Burgesses petitioned the Board of Trade to allow Virginia to annex Kentucky and to the Kanawha–Ohio junction in 1769, their petition was denied.[8]

The rights of Virginia on the upper Ohio were contested by Pennsylvania. At Fort Stanwyx, Johnson allowed a group of Philadelphia merchants, led by Thomas and Samuel Wharton, to buy 2,400,000 acres from the Indians. Samuel Wharton went to London seeking Parliamentary approval. George Mercer (John Mercer's son) for the Ohio Company and Arthur Lee for the Mississippi Company pressed their claims in London. Lord Hillsborough, Secretary for American Affairs, denied all these claims, citing the 1763 Proclamation.[9] He had previously (January 3, 1771) assured Virginia that attention would be given to equitable claims of Ohio Company settlers and war veterans.[10]

Britain's Secret Policy

While most people attributed the Proclamation to Pontiac's War, the origin of the policy was unrelated to it. In 1772, the Board of Trade wrote the Privy Council: "We take leave to remind your Lordships of that principle, which was adopted by the Board, and approved and confirmed by his Majesty, immediately after the Treaty of Paris, viz. the confining the western extent of settlement to such a distance from the sea coast, as that those settlements should lie within the reach of the trade and commerce of this kingdom, upon which the strength and riches of it depend, and also of the exercise of the authority and jurisdiction which was conceived to be necessary for the preservation of the colonies in due subordinance to, and dependence upon the mother country."[11] This was the same policy behind the other Acts of 1763–1764, which strengthened imperial control to keep the colonies in subordination to Britain and enrich it even at the expense of the colonies. Like Ireland.

Apparently, neither the original nor a copy of the 1763 document from the Board of Trade to the Privy Council that was approved by the King has been found, and it may have been lost or deliberately destroyed at a later date. Its existence and contents are evidenced by the 1772 document from the Board of Trade to the Privy Council. That evidence is sufficient since it is inconceivable that the Board of Trade would have misstated the record only nine years later. The 1772 document, which has been found, mentions the submission of the 1763 document to the King, and his approval of it. It would be equally inconceivable that a radical change in policy of the nature of the 1763 Proclamation would have been submitted by the Board of Trade directly to the King, rather than being vetted through his Privy Council first. It may be safely stated that the Board of Trade's recommendation in 1763 was directed to the Privy Council, which recommended it to the King, who then gave his approval. The Board of Trade's 1772 report to the Privy Council may, or may not, have been seen by the King, since it was providing information for the Privy Council's consideration regarding a possible change in policy, and apparently was opposing a proposed change. If the original of the 1763 policy adoption and recommendation by the Board of Trade was indeed deliberately destroyed, thinking to cover the tracks of the origin of such a disastrous policy, the later description of that paper by the 1772 document was spared by oversight, since the person doing so may not have known of, or had access to, the later document.

The Hovering Act of 1763

In 1763, Parliament passed an Act providing for seizure of dutiable goods in large vessels found "hovering" off the coast of North America, presumably waiting for an opportunity to slip past Customs. The dutiable goods could be seized and sold, and the proceeds divided among the officers and crew. Twenty naval vessels, recently released for this assignment by peace with France and Spain, were posted to North America for Customs duty, promptly followed by several seizures.[12]

The Currency Act of 1764

British merchants were disturbed by the amount of paper money issued by all the colonies, especially when colonial legislation made it legal tender, which the merchant was required to accept in payment at its face value. They objected, even after Virginia's Assembly had required a 25 percent discount for payment in paper.

In April 1764, Parliament passed a Currency Act prohibiting the issuance of "legal tender" paper money after September 1, 1764. Paper could still be used to pay public debts, but private debts were payable only in specie (gold and silver), also called "sterling." Because of an acute shortage of specie, the Assembly had issued non-legal tender paper in 1759 and 1761.[13]

The effect, with the Proclamation, was to reduce further the amount of currency in circulation, bringing on a reduction of credit and dramatic drops in the value of land and slaves.

The Sugar Act of 1764

Effective September 29, 1764, the tax on importation of sugar, molasses, and rum from foreign colonies was extended. In November 1764, the Customs Board notified all Customs officers in North America to enforce the tax or be removed. The Ministry was buying the votes of fifty to sixty Members of Parliament with West Indies interests, a bloc whose loss would oust the Ministry of George Grenville. The primary targets were in New England.[14]

The American Act of 1764

The primary target, again, was the smugglers of New England, but Virginia suffered collateral damage. The Act imposed heavy duties on wine from Madeira, the Azores, and the Canaries—colonies of Portugal and Spain, not necessarily involved in the wars with France; the wines were primarily imported by the Virginia planters.[15]

Worse, the Act prohibited a vessel from carrying freight to America unless the entire shipment was loaded in Britain. A vessel with goods from the Continent could not be "topped off" in Britain without unloading the foreign goods, paying duty on them, and then reloading them. Still worse, no vessel could sail from one colony to another without papers from Customs. Every vessel must give at least £1,000 bond for each trip or be subject to seizure and forfeiture, including small vessels sailing from one colony to another.[16] Many Virginia planters had small vessels of their own, employed on intercolonial trade, especially in Chesapeake Bay. Some great planters had ships engaged in the trans-Atlantic trade with Britain. Finally, all suits for penalties could be brought in admiralty courts, without jury trial.

The cost of Customs "papers" and giving bond for each voyage was in addition to the additional expense in lost time getting those papers from a Customs office at a location remote from the "port," usually a planter's personal wharf. These costs were particularly burdensome on small boats carrying small cargos on short intercolonial voyages.

The most oppressive features of the Act were those encouraging corruption. The Act gave existing colonial admiralty courts jurisdiction to hear forfeiture cases and also created a new Admiralty Court in Halifax, Nova Scotia. It had jurisdiction over condemnations and trials of vessels seized for violations of the Act anywhere in the North American colonies. The burden of proof to show compliance with the Act was placed on the owner of the vessel, who had to transport his witnesses to Halifax. The naval commander who seized the vessel received one-half the proceeds of its sale if forfeited for Customs violations. The naval officers were exempted from liability for unlawful seizures.[17] Because admiralty courts had no jury trials, all these issues would be resolved by the Royal Judge. The potential for corruption so richly rewarded and the consequent animosity it would arouse is obvious. The court in Halifax opened in October 1764. The Ministry must have had second thoughts about this act, because only one case was ever filed in the Halifax court in 1765 for seizure outside of Nova Scotia. In 1768, the Halifax Admiralty Court for all of North America was abolished. It was replaced with four district Admiralty Courts in Halifax, Boston, Philadelphia, and Charleston. They had jurisdiction over ordinary admiralty cases, offenses against acts of trade and revenue, and appeals from colonial admiralty courts.

By 1763–1764, Randolph was an important member of the governing group, mostly James and York River men, led by Speaker John Robinson. While they did not like the new Acts, they regarded them as laws in regulation of imperial trade and therefore constitutional.

5. Britain's Post-War Policy Toward the Colonies

They could, and would, work within the system that had in the past allowed them to obtain relief from the authorities in London. They certainly did not discern any malicious or oppressive intent in these Acts. Rather, New England's smuggling was notorious, and the Acts apparently were trying to deal with that problem by using a sledgehammer.

Richard Henry Lee may have been the first prominent Virginian to detect the overall policy behind these Acts of 1763–1764. On May 31, 1764, he wrote a friend, "many late determinations … seem to prove a resolution to oppress North America with the iron hand of power." For his prescience, he became labeled a "radical."[18]

6

The Stamp Act

In March 1764, the Chancellor of the Exchequer, George Grenville, proposed a Stamp Tax to help pay the cost of the war and also the costs of administration and defense of the colonies. The bill itself was not offered by the Ministry in the House of Commons until February 1765, after the Ministry had gathered more information. Consequently, the details of the proposed bill were not available until the bill was filed, but enough was known to arouse grave concern. The constitutional issue was immediately apparent. Virginia denied the right of Parliament to impose an internal tax or to legislate regarding internal police powers of the colony; these fields were deemed the exclusive field of action of the General Assembly. On the merits of the grounds proposed by Grenville as justification for the tax, Virginia pointed out its own great sacrifices and large war debt. Furthermore, with the expulsion of the French from North America, there was no serious defense problem other than the Indians. The proposed tax was obviously part of the program of legislation of 1763 and 1764. While the Hovering Act, the Sugar Act, and the American Act affected Virginia to a lesser degree than they did New England, the Proclamation of 1763 and the Currency Act had major impacts on Virginia. The Stamp Act would be in addition to these.

One of the moments of high drama in the story of the Stamp Act is, or was, shown in the film at the Visitor Center in Williamsburg, explaining the significance of Williamsburg to the non-historian visitor. The film shows a portly Peyton Randolph storming out of the House of Burgesses, declaring: "By God, I would have given 500 guineas for a single vote" (which would have tied the vote on Patrick Henry's fifth resolution and allowed Speaker Robinson to break the tie and to defeat it). This correct portrayal of Randolph's position in May 1765 would

35

Capitol, exterior, Williamsburg (Colonial Williamsburg Foundation, No. D2005-TEG-0412-028f).

appear to justify Jefferson's inclusion of Randolph in his list of the "less ardent" leaders of Virginia, those called by recent historians "the conservatives."[1] There is no question that Randolph did indeed oppose Henry's epochal resolutions, but it is important to understand why he did so. As another leader on Jefferson's list of the "less ardent," Edmund Pendleton, also labeled by modern writers as a "conservative," wrote to John Madison (father of James Madison) on February 13, 1766: "Not one in a thousand" would admit the stamps. "I … having taken an oath to decide according to law, shall never consider that act as such for want of power (I mean constitutional authority) in the Parliament to pass it."[2] As we shall see, Randolph was among Pendleton's estimate of 999 out of 1,000 who denied the constitutionality of the Act.

July 1764: Protest by Committee of Correspondence

In July 1764, the Committee of Correspondence met to consider its notification from Edward Montague, the General Assembly's agent

House of Burgesses, Capitol, Williamsburg (Colonial Williamsburg Foundation, No. D2002-BKT-0618-032-33).

in London, regarding Grenville's intent to bring in a bill for a stamp tax in the colonies. The first public figure in Virginia to denounce and attack the Stamp Act was Landon Carter, a member of the Committee.[3] The General Assembly not being in session nor scheduled to meet until October, the Committee of Correspondence drafted a protest to send to Montague. Randolph was on the Committee, which met in Williamsburg. The actual draft was prepared by George Wythe and Robert Carter Nicholas, approved by the Committee, and sent to Montague for delivery in London. Not knowing the scope of the proposed tax, the protest was founded both on Virginia's

John Robinson, John Wollaston, 1755-1758 oil on canvas (Colonial Williamsburg Foundation, No. TC1990-0019).

burden under its own war debt and the injustice of its being taxed for the war a second time and on the constitutional ground. In measured language, it stated the precedents against Parliament's right to levy an internal tax in Virginia. Finally, it even suggested a way of raising revenue by requisition, as was done during the war, which would be a constitutional method in the event Parliament was determined to raise more revenue.[4] No answer was received from the Ministry.

October 30, 1764: Petitions by General Assembly

The General Assembly convened on October 30, 1764. On November 1, a message from the Massachusetts House and, on November 7, a letter from Montague, the General Assembly's agent (not the Governor's agent), were laid on the table in the House of Burgesses, allowing all members to study them. On November 13, the House resolved itself into a Committee of the Whole to consider these messages. The rules for the Committee of the Whole allow a much more informal and free-ranging debate than during a formal session of the House. All resolutions dealing with this subject would have been referred to the Committee on Propositions and Grievances, of which Randolph was chairman, which then would have drafted the resolution for appointment of a special committee and reported that resolution to the House. Resolutions were passed authorizing an address to the King and memorials to the House of Commons and the House of Lords. The Speaker appointed Randolph as chairman of the committee, with Richard Henry Lee, Landon Carter, George Wythe, Edmund Pendleton, Benjamin Harrison, Archibald Cary, and John Fleming as members. Richard Bland was added three days later, probably at the request of Randolph and his committee. When the committee's draft resolutions were reported to the House, the Committee of the Whole debated them for a week. The drafts reviewed the grants to Virginia and the precedents, establishing Virginia's right through its General Assembly, subject to approval by the Crown or its representative Governor, to determine the internal taxes to be laid upon its people, and the lack of any such right in Parliament. "The people are not subject to any taxes but such as are laid on them by their own consent or by those who are legally appointed to represent them." If Parliament has the right to tax the colonies, "the colonies are but the slaves of Britain." This language was adopted by the Committee of the Whole. The drafts also suggested dire effects upon commercial relations between Britain and Virginia, should an unconstitutional stamp tax be levied. A strong minority wanted even harsher language, and Randolph was among those who opposed stronger terms. The majority did not want to offend Parliament or the Ministry too much, since Virginia had a long history of moderating the actions in London by persistent, reasonable petitions. The address to the King was approved, and the memorials to the Commons and the Lords were amended in minor respects. All three were then passed by the House and sent to the Council. Randolph and most members of the committee then met with members of the Council, who required amendments as a condition to their consent. Those amendments having been negotiated and made, the Council concurred on December 18, 1764, and all three petitions were forwarded to Montague by the Committee of Correspondence as Acts of the General Assembly. The General Assembly recessed on December 21 until May 1, 1765. The cover letter to Montague said that the Committee of Correspondence were aware that the Commons had refused to accept petitions from some other colonies. If the Crown, Commons, or Lords refused to accept Virginia's petitions, he should have them printed and distributed.[5]

The General Assembly had spent most of its time for seven weeks on the issue of the proposed stamp tax, whose scope was still unknown. The burden of this effort was especially heavy on Randolph. As chairman of the Committee on Propositions and Grievances, he had steered the House's concern and anger into the time-honored channel of petitions. As chairman of the special committee, he struggled for days within the committee to restrain members like Lee and Fleming to produce petitions that would not cause a reflexive slamming of the door in London, a refusal even to accept the petition, as the Commons had refused the petitions of other colonies. Reread the language quoted above, which was reported to the House by his committee. This is the watered-down version that Randolph was able to keep from being even stronger in tone! Randolph then shepherded the drafts through the

Committee of the Whole, convinced or held off the minority in the House who favored even stronger language, and then negotiated the language of the petitions with the Council, finally obtaining their consent so that London could see that the petitions were those of the entire colony, including the Councilors who were the Crown's own appointees. Finally, as a member of the Committee of Correspondence, he participated in drafting instructions to the General Assembly's agent in London. The efforts of the General Assembly, and particularly those of the Burgesses, were tremendous. But the pressure on Randolph, requiring great skill and patience, was unremitting for seven weeks. The fact that he was chairman of the special committee that asserted the rights of Virginia so forthrightly can leave no doubt that he was indeed one of Pendleton's 999 who believed that the constitutional rights of Virginia were being threatened. Unlike most of the Burgesses, he had lived and studied in England, been admitted to the Bar there, and had spent more time there successfully representing the Burgesses in the Pistole Fee dispute. His father had done the same before him. He felt that he knew what would work and what would not, and very few, if any, of the other Burgesses had anything like his experience. It is notable that he supported language as provocative as that quoted, but he did not wish to alienate potential friends of Virginia in London.

Terms and Passage of the Stamp Act

The Ministry's bill was filed in the Commons in February 1765. Its scope was breathtaking. Virtually all legal actions were taxed repeatedly at many different levels. There was a tax on the license to practice law. The tax must be paid on every land survey, every deed, every promissory note, every mortgage, every insurance policy, every bond, every ship charter, every customs clearance, and every bill of lading. A heavy levy was made on communications within the colonies. Every copy of every newspaper must have a half-pence stamp affixed, and every newspaper advertisement must pay a two-shilling tax. Pamphlets and almanacs were taxed. Access to the courts was heavily taxed. Each sheet of legal paper must have a three-pence stamp. In addition, each chancery pleading was taxed one shilling six pence, every probate proceeding five shillings, four shillings for every judgment or decree, ten shillings for a writ of appeal, and two shillings for bail. Entertainment was taxed. A pair of dice was taxed ten shillings, and taxes were placed on every deck of playing cards and every liquor license. (The most popular wines had already been subjected to exorbitant duties by the 1764 American Act.) The crowning blow was that the tax must be paid in specie——gold and silver[6]—of which there was very little in the colonies, which they had alleviated with paper money and, in Virginia, with tobacco warehouse receipts; new issues of the former were no longer legal tender for any private debts due to the 1764 Currency Act. People said there was not enough specie in the colonies to pay the stamp tax for a single year, and they were probably right. (For readers who are not familiar with British currency prior to Britain's adoption of the metric system, one guinea is one pound one shilling; one pound is twenty shillings; one crown is five shillings; a half-crown is two and one-half shillings; one florin is two shillings; one shilling is twelve pence; and there were half-pence and farthings, one-quarter pence.) To put the amount of these taxes in perspective, recall that the price of purchase of 100 acres from the Crown was five shillings.

In his presentation to the Commons, Grenville boasted that he had not read any of the colonial petitions and protests. Most colonial petitions were deemed too inflammatory to be presented, but the Commons heard Virginia's petition, though it voted to reject it "by a great majority." William Pitt, the former prime minister who had successfully conducted the Seven Years' War, opposed the bill, but he was sick and unable to do much. The resolution approving the bill passed the Commons "with less opposition than a turnpike bill" on a vote of 245–49. It was accepted by the Lords and approved by the King on March 22, 1765. The Act was to be effective on November 1, 1765. While the Ministry's intent was not fully disclosed, the Secretary to the Treasurer, Thomas Whatley, wrote on February 9, 1765, "The great measure of the session is the American Stamp Act; I give it the appellation of *a great measure* on account of the important point it establishes, the right of Parliament to lay an internal tax upon the colonies" (emphasis in original).[7]

May 1765 Session: Patrick Henry's Resolutions

Soon after the General Assembly convened on May 1, 1765, they learned the terms of the bill from a May 2 edition of a Maryland newspaper, which printed an unofficial copy of the bill's text and unofficial news of its passage. If the bill had passed, it was law and too late to object. If it had not yet passed, intemperate action might result in its passage or prevent its repeal. So the leaders of the Burgesses waited for official news.

A new member from Hanover County, Patrick Henry, met with three other western members and prepared their own legislative offensive. The other three were John Fleming, George Johnston, and Colonel Robert Munford. As the end of the session approached and the session's business had been done, most of the Burgesses left town, including George Washington, Edmund Pendleton, and Landon Carter. Richard Henry Lee had not attended any of the session. On about May 28, a letter was received from Montague enclosing a copy of the Resolution of the Commons, which had been agreed to by the Lords, but the letter was sent before the King signed it. There was thus no official notice of the bill's becoming law, nor whether there was any response to the General Assembly's petitions.[8]

Only 39 Burgesses and the Speaker out of 116 members were present on May 29 when George Johnston of Alexandria rose and moved to have the House resolve itself into a Committee of the Whole to consider the Stamp Act. His motion passed. Speaker Robinson stepped down, and Randolph took the Chair. John Randolph, Clerk of the House,

Patrick Henry, **Thomas Sully, 1815 oil on canvas, after a miniature from life by Lawrence Sully (Colonial Williamsburg Foundation, No. 1998-0290).**

removed the mace, signifying that the House itself was not in session. Henry presented five resolutions with a preamble. The short preamble, reciting the necessity of responding to the Commons' claim of power to tax, was eliminated in the debate. The five resolutions were: (1) Colonists have always enjoyed all liberties (added in debate), privileges, franchises, and immunities of people of Great Britain. (2) By charters from James I, colonists have all the rights of subjects born in Great Britain. (3) Taxation of the people by themselves or those chosen to represent them who know what taxes the people can bear and the easiest mode of raising them "and are equally affected by such Taxes themselves" is the distinguishing characteristic of British freedom and without which the ancient Constitution cannot exist. (4) Colonists of Virginia have enjoyed the right of being governed by their Assembly in matters of taxes and internal police. (5) The General Assembly of Virginia have the only right to lay taxes and impositions and attempts to vest such power elsewhere has the tendency to destroy British as well as American freedom. The resolutions were only one-fifth the length of the petitions sent to London six months earlier. Robinson, Bland, Wythe, and Nicholas argued that the resolutions were repetitious of those previously passed and were likely to irritate Parliament and the Ministry, thereby either assuring the bill's approval or hindering efforts to repeal it. They said that they agreed with the first four resolutions but deplored the immoderation of their tone. A few members admitted the right of taxation by the Crown and Parliament but deplored its application, and a few others denied their power to tax but said it had to be endured until repealed. Munford and Fleming spoke in favor of the resolutions "with special vigor." Henry denied the right of any but the General Assembly to tax.[9]

All five resolutions were reported by the Committee of the Whole to the House. On May 30, with the Speaker again in the Chair, Randolph read the Resolutions to the House. Debate was resumed, and Randolph added his voice to the opponents that day. The Resolutions were voted on in the order presented. The first three were passed on votes of 22–17. The fourth Resolution was amended to make a correction pointed out by the opponents, adding "with the approbation of their Sovereign or his substitute." It then passed 22–17.

In the debate on the fifth Resolution, Henry concluded his oration, saying, "Tarquin and Caesar each had his Brutus, Charles I his Cromwell, and George III." At this point, Robinson interrupted him from the Chair, shouting "Treason!" Henry concluded, "may profit by their example." Robinson then ruled that the words were treasonable. Henry apologized and avowed loyalty to the King, and the treason issue dropped. After further debate, the Resolution carried 20–19. Thomas Jefferson, then a student at William and Mary College observing the debate, recorded Randolph's irate wish for one more vote.[10]

Henry, being a new member of the Burgesses, thought the matter was settled and left town. But the House had not adjourned. Randolph searched the House's journals for a precedent to expunge. On May 31, Robinson called the House to order. He refused to recognize a quorum call and then recognized Randolph, who moved to strike all five Resolutions passed the day before. The motions to strike the first four Resolutions failed. The motion to strike the fifth Resolution tied, and Robinson broke the tie by voting to strike the Resolution.

The aftermath—the rallying of opinion in Virginia and the encouragement to resistance elsewhere—proved that Henry had the better grasp of the political realities of the situation that day than the leaders of the Burgesses did. Randolph and the leaders were playing to a London audience, which was not listening and, unbeknownst to them, was not going to listen. Henry was speaking to the people at home, the correct approach, as his instincts told him.

A copy of the five Resolutions passed by the Burgesses on May 30 was already on its way north before Randolph's motions to expunge revoked the fifth Resolution. It was circulated in Pennsylvania and New York as Virginia's response to passage of the Stamp Act. Someone else sent north that night a copy of the full list of seven Resolutions drafted by Henry and his three collaborators, including the last two which were not even offered, which was erroneously published in New England as the action of Virginia. The last two resolutions stated that the people were not bound to obedience to the unconstitutional Stamp Act and that any person who asserts otherwise is an enemy of Virginia. James Otis, a leader of the radicals in Boston, and Benjamin Franklin of Pennsylvania both criticized Virginia's purported actions as being too rash.[11]

Resistance and Repeal

Nevertheless, Maryland, Pennsylvania, Rhode Island, and Massachusetts passed resolutions during the summer of 1765. While Virginia's protest was based on its "rights," Massachusetts based its protest as a matter of "privilege."[12] The distinction in the basis of the two colonies' claims indicates the great degree of unity in Virginia and the lack thereof in Massachusetts, as events would subsequently prove. The Massachusetts legislature issued a call for a Congress of all the colonies to meet in New York in October. Nine colonies sent representatives, but Virginia did not appear. Governor Fauquier had dissolved the General Assembly and would not call an election for the new Burgesses, which could have elected delegates. The Congress sent a petition, declaring that only colonial legislatures could levy internal taxes and that a provision in the Act giving the Admiralty Court in Halifax, Nova Scotia, jurisdiction over Stamp Tax disputes was also unconstitutional.[13]

The Committee of Correspondence initially did not send a copy of the four Resolutions that had not been expunged to their agent in London. But with the last three resolutions being attributed to Virginia in London, Randolph and Wythe finally sent Montague an official copy in September, which had only the first four Resolutions. They sought to distance the colony from both the fifth, expunged resolution and from the other two, not even offered.[14]

Governor Francis Fauquier. **Francis Fauquier (c. 1704–68), Lieutenant Governor of Virginia in the American colonies, Benjamin Wilson (1721–88), oil on canvas, c. 1757 (Coram in the care of the Foundling Museum, London / Bridgman Images).**

6. The Stamp Act

Because the Burgesses did not meet between May 31 and the effective date of the Act, November 1, the resistance was uncoordinated in Virginia. In Virginia, as throughout the colonies, many merchants and individual planters notified their London connections that no more goods would be ordered for delivery after November 1. Lawyers and county judges announced that no proceedings would be taken which required a stamp. Parades were held, effigies were burned, and groups calling themselves "Associations" or "Sons of Liberty" gathered to intimidate the minority. Pressure was brought to bear in all the colonies on the appointed distributors of the stamps, demanding their resignations. Massachusetts experienced the most violence. On August 26, the Massachusetts Lieutenant Governor's personal home was utterly destroyed, stripped to bare walls inside, and all the windows and doors were broken out.[15] The distributors elsewhere had resigned, and mobs prevented the stamps from being unloaded from the ships.

In Virginia, "Associations" were widely formed. The "Associators" adopted resolutions condemning the Stamp Act and resolving not to accept its legality and not to trade with Britain until its repeal. By the terms of the Associations, the resolutions were voluntary acts of the "Associators," not legally binding on others, since they carried no legislative authority from any level of government. Many Associations bound their members to remonstrate with any in the colony who acted contrary to the resolutions. In September 1765, Richard Henry Lee led a protest to the Westmoreland County Courthouse. Lee had dressed his slaves in red coats, cocked hats, and boots to copy John Wilkes's followers in Britain, described hereafter. One hundred citizens adopted the "Westmoreland Resolves." They burned in effigy Grenville and George Mercer, who was appointed Stamp Agent for Virginia. They complained of the Governor's dissolution of the General Assembly, the source of their legitimate taxation. They resolved that British subjects, including Virginians, could be tried only by their peers and taxed only by a Parliament in which they had elected representatives. They promised "to preserve the laws, the peace and good order of the Colony as far as is consistent with the preservation of our rights and liberties." The Westmoreland Resolves, drawn by Lee to state Virginia's protest in vigorous terms, were widely admired and copied throughout Virginia and other colonies.[16] (Lee was later damaged by the revelation that he had sought assistance from friends in London to obtain the post of Stamp Agent for himself. That effort was made before the text was known and before he knew the tax was to be payable in specie. Lee admitted his error and disavowed it, but there is little question that some people forever regarded him as an opportunist.)

In February 1766, Archibald Ritchie, Lee's neighbor in the adjoining county, said that he would buy stamps so that his ships could sail. Lee led 400 men to descend on Ritchie's plantation. Under their threats, Ritchie made a formal written apology and vow not to use any stamped paper.[17] This type of action, repeated elsewhere on a smaller scale and led by less prominent men, demonstrated the true intent of the resolutions' nature purportedly binding only on the Associators and the resolutions to remonstrate with non–Associators. The effectiveness of the voluntary Associations rested upon the implicit threat of violence against anyone willing to accept the Stamp Act.

The most prominent "remonstrance" was that made to George Mercer, a Virginian well regarded, George Mason's first cousin, who was awarded the post of Stamp Agent largely as a reward for his war service. When he arrived in Williamsburg on October 30, the stamps were still on a warship in the York River. The town was full of people who had arrived for opening of the General Court

Richard Henry Lee, **colorized version of a 19th century engraving by Johnson, Fry & Co., made from an original painting by Alonzo Chappel (courtesy DuPont Library, Stratford Hall, Stratford, Virginia).**

and the fall transaction of business. As he approached Christiana Campbell's Tavern, where he was to dine upon his arrival, a large crowd gathered around him, protesting and demanding that he resign. A group of leading men gathered on the front porch feared for his safety and pushed through the crowd to surround him and lead him to safety inside. Governor Fauquier described the event: "This concourse of people I should call a mob, did I not know that it was chiefly, if not altogether, composed of gentlemen of property in the Colony, some of them at the head of their respective counties." The next day Mercer announced that he would "not proceed further with the Act until I receive further orders from England and not then until I receive the assent of the General Assembly of this colony."[18] The next day, the effective day of the Act, November 1, 1765, the General Court opened its session with the Governor, the Council, and the Attorney General, Randolph, in attendance. The Court was formally announced open to

Christiana Campbell's Tavern, Williamsburg (Colonial Williamsburg Foundation, No. D2013-BTL-0503-1184).

conduct its business, but not a single lawyer or litigant appeared. Governor Fauquier finally adjourned the Court until April 1766.[19] Pendleton, who was also Caroline County Judge, opened his court but conducted only that business that did not require stamps. Some county judges did not open their courts at all that fall and winter. In February 1766, Pendleton opened his court, declared the Stamp Act unconstitutional, and conducted business for which the Act required stamps. A number of other county courts did the same.[20]

Unlike some governors in other colonies, Governor Fauquier allowed ships to come and go without stamps, so Virginia suffered less that winter than some other colonies. He received intimations from London that the Act would be repealed, and he passed this on to leaders in Virginia. Pitt spoke powerfully against the Stamp Act and the Ministry. "This kingdom has no right to lay a tax upon the colonies.... The Americans are the sons, not the bastards, of England. The Commons of America, represented in their several assemblies, have ever been in possession of the exercise of this, their constitutional right, of giving and granting their own money. They would have been slaves if they had not enjoyed it."[21] Did Pitt deliberately quote Virginia's petition that, if Parliament had the right to tax the colonies, "the colonies are but the slaves of Britain"? The Grenville Ministry fell as a result largely of the pressure of the London merchants. The merchants lobbied the new Rockingham Whig Ministry. Pitt urged the new Whig Ministry to repeal the Act. He argued that it was unnecessary and unfair to impose the cost of defense and

Edmund Pendleton, Thomas Sully, 19th century oil on canvas, after a miniature by William Mercer (1773–1850) (Virginia Historical Society, No. 1851.2).

administration upon the colonies because the policies already imposed on them resulted in an annual £2,000,000 profit to Britain, an enormous sum. The Commons passed a resolution for repeal 275–167 and voted to repeal the Stamp Act and to pass the Declaratory Act on March 4, 1766. Both were offered in the Lords on the next day. The Lords approved repeal on March 11, and the Act was signed by the King on March 18, 1766.[22] On May 2, the *Virginia Gazette* published news of its repeal.

The Sons of Liberty disbanded. Many Virginians remained loyal to the King and to Parliament. They ascribed the Stamp Act to bad advisers who had personal motives of private gain. Although the petitions of the colonists had been backed up with unusual vigor on this occasion, once again colonial protest of disadvantageous actions in London had procured relief. The Virginians were given intimations of further relief to come, some of which did, as witnessed by the gradual reduction in area covered by the Proclamation Line in 1768 and 1769.

There is no question that Randolph believed the Stamp Act to be unconstitutional, evidenced by the strong statement of that position in the December 1764 resolutions of the General Assembly, which could only have come out of the special committee with his approval as its chairman. Randolph had experience with the drill in London— the revision of disadvantageous governmental actions through patient remonstrance and solicitation of the colony's friends and business associates in London. The cover letter of the Committee of Correspondence forwarding the petitions to Montague says as much, telling him to have the petitions printed and distributed if the Commons or Lords did not accept them. In other words, appeal to Virginia's friends and to British merchants whose businesses were about to be injured. Randolph was obviously unhappy to see what he regarded as intemperate language adopted in May 1765. Henry's language could alienate Virginia's friends and encourage adoption or prevent repeal of the Stamp Act or its revision into something acceptable. Thus, the great labor of Randolph and others in November–December 1764, taking essentially the same position but in less offensive form, was undone by Henry's Resolutions. The Henry Resolutions also weakened Virginia's position; the December 1764 petitions were by the entire General Assembly, while Henry's were from the Burgesses only. The Councilors appointed by the Crown did not join in Henry's. Randolph was furious that all this was accomplished over his opposition by a young new member of no family or significant political connection from a western county. It was a great humiliation to Randolph personally. In a sense, Randolph's position was correct. While it was new that the remonstrances were more widespread and more violent than ever before, they did result in repeal of the Act. What was also new was that the Board of Trade had already resolved, and the Privy Council and King had agreed, that the colonies were to be restricted to the Atlantic seaboard, to be held in absolute subservience to Britain and subjected to internal taxation for Britain's benefit without the colonies' consent. A large new Ireland was intended. Richard Henry Lee and Patrick Henry had correctly divined London's intent, and Randolph had not yet done so.

The Declaratory Act: 1766

Simultaneously with repeal of the Stamp Act, Parliament passed a Declaratory Act, as witnessed by the repeal of the Stamp Act and the Declaratory Act not being offered in the Lords until the day after the Commons had passed both. It provided that the Crown and Parliament "had, hath and of right ought to have the full power and authority to make laws and statutes of sufficient force and validity to bind the Colonies and people of America, subjects of the Crown of Great Britain, in all cases whatsoever." The Declaratory Act was the concession given to obtain the votes of enough Lords to repeal the Stamp Act in the House of Lords.[23]

Pitt somehow found this language ambiguous and construed it in favor of the colonies. Most colonists believed it to be a face-saving device rather than an expression of future intent.[24] We are not the first generation to refuse to apply the correct name to events we do not wish to deal with. While notice of the passage of the Declaratory Act arrived with notice of repeal of the Stamp Act, the relief over repeal was so great that few indeed were willing to gear up again for another struggle so soon. And in Virginia, the attention of the colony was refocused elsewhere days after notice of repeal.

Richard Bland's Pamphlet

As asserted by Pendleton, "Not one in a thousand would admit the stamps."[25] The Virginians were overwhelmingly united in their belief that internal taxes could be levied in Virginia only with the consent of the Burgesses. This was their constitutional right. This unity of conviction was the source of Virginia's strength and was unmatched in the other colonies. How had this come about?

In the first instance, this was the rule and practice which had prevailed during the lifetime of every living Virginian. It had been the rule and practice in the colony since time immemorial, as far back as anyone could remember or had heard tell. At the outset of the constitutional struggle with Great Britain, their belief in the right of the Burgesses to consent, and to withhold consent, to any internal tax was fundamental. This was the crux of the Pistole Fee dispute between the Burgesses and Governor Dinwiddie in 1752–1754. As the General Assembly asserted in its 1764 petitions on the Stamp Act, if Parliament could levy internal taxes in Virginia, "the colonies are but the slaves of Britain."[26] Virginia

RICHARD BLAND
by Susan Brown
Patriot, statesman, planter for whom Richard Bland College of the College of William and Mary in Virginia is named. Founded by the General Assembly in 1960 in Petersburg, Va.

Richard Bland, 1975 oil painting by Susan Brown, after a portrait of Bland as one of the Burgesses shown listening to Patrick Henry's speech against the Stamp Act in an 1851 painting by Peter Frederick Rothermel (courtesy Richard Bland College of the College of William and Mary, South Prince George, Virginia).

was older than all the other colonies and much older than any colony outside of New England. Virginians knew that this had been the constitutional position of the Burgesses as far as it could be traced, well over 100 years.

It was Richard Bland, the lawyer who assembled the largest collection of legal records pertaining to Virginia, called by Jefferson "the Virginia Antiquary," who handed Virginians the historical record with which to defend their position.

In 1766, Bland published in Williamsburg, and offered for sale in London also, a pamphlet entitled *An Inquiry into the Rights of the British Colonies.*[27] The pamphlet was directed against an anonymous pamphlet published in Britain asserting Parliament's right to legislate for Virginia on the theory that Virginia was "virtually represented" in Parliament in the same manner as 90 percent of the inhabitants of the Kingdom, who also did not have the right to vote for any member of the House of Commons. Bland first responded in terms that would apply to all the colonies, based on natural law and John Locke's theories of social compact.

He then recited the basis of Virginia's constitutional rights, which were particular to Virginia alone. In doing so, he laid out the constitutional history of Virginia in terms that could be recited and cited by any Virginian.

He showed how the colony, planted by the finances and efforts of the Virginia Company and the individual settlers "without receiving the least assistance from the English government," in 1621 established a General Assembly consisting of the Governor, Council, and Burgesses, elected by freeholders as their representatives, as the legislative authority.[28] James I dissolved the Virginia Company in 1624, causing much confusion, which was resolved in 1634. The Privy Council gave the assurance of Charles I that "all their Estates, Trades, Freedom and Privileges should be enjoyed by them in as extensive a Manner as they enjoyed them before the recalling the Company's Patent [by James I]." The rights of the Burgesses before 1624 were thereby confirmed by the Crown in 1634.[29]

The General Assembly in 1642 opposed an effort to have Parliament restore the Virginia Company, and the colony recognized Charles

6. The Stamp Act

I and his government throughout the English Civil War. (New England supported Parliament and, later, the military dictatorship of Oliver Cromwell and his son, Richard.) Following the execution of Charles I in 1649, the General Assembly proclaimed Charles II as King in Virginia.[30] In 1652, Parliament sent warships and transports to Virginia to reduce it to obedience. Governor Sir William Berkeley called out the militia and negotiated with two Virginians serving as plenipotentiary Commissioners for Parliament. Berkeley successfully negotiated a peaceful delivery of executive authority to the Commissioners, preservation of the existing political order, a general amnesty for opposition to Parliament, non-debarkation of the troops, at least a year's protection for the Established Church and its ministers, and preservation of the right of private citizens to own arms, ammunition, and powder.

Of special importance for the issues arising a century later were these four enumerated articles: (1) The inhabitants of Virginia "shall have and enjoy such freedoms and privileges as belong to the freeborn people of England." (2) "The Grand [General] Assembly as formerly shall convene and transact the affairs of Virginia, wherein nothing is to be acted or done contrary to the government of the Commonwealth of England and the laws there established...." (4) "Virginia shall have and enjoy the ancient bounds and limits granted by the charters of the former Kings...." (8) "Virginia shall

Governor Sir William Berkeley, **Sir Peter Lely, oil on canvas, c. 1662 (Berkeley Castle Charitable Trust, Berkeley, Gloucestershire, United Kingdom).**

be free from all taxes, customs and impositions whatsoever, and none to be imposed on them without consent of the Grand Assembly."[31]

Pursuant to the Articles of Surrender, two successive Cromwellian Governors were elected by the cautious Burgesses. Following Oliver Cromwell's death, during the succession of his son, Richard, as "Protector" or military dictator, in January 1660 the Burgesses and Council elected Berkeley as Governor pro tempore. He convened the General Assembly in March, which elected him as Governor. His election effectively abrogated the surrender to the Commonwealth contrary to the 1652 Articles of Surrender, which prohibited Sir William from political activity in Virginia. Royalist government was thereby effectively restored in Virginia. This was almost three months before the Restoration of Charles II in London.[32]

During the reign of Charles II, "when it was thought necessary to establish a permanent revenue for the support of government in Virginia, the King did not apply to the English Parliament, but to the General Assembly, and sent over an Act, under the Great Seal of England, by which it was enacted by the King's Most Excellent Majesty, by and with the consent of the General Assembly...."[33]

In 1676, Virginia protested the Navigation Act of Charles II as impinging on its free trade. The King issued a Declaration under his Privy Seal, that "impositions or taxes ought not be laid upon the inhabitants and proprietors of the colony but by the common consent of the General Assembly, except such impositions as the Parliament should lay on the commodities imported into England from the colony." A charter was then issued under the Great Seal securing this right to the colony.[34]

Bland's pamphlet confirmed the Virginians in their conviction that their constitutional position—no internal tax without the consent of the Burgesses—was secured not only by long-standing custom, tradition, and practice, but also that the most solemn acts of the successive governments of England had guaranteed these rights over the period from 1624 to date. Bland's service to the cause of Virginia's liberty can hardly be exaggerated. As the struggle intensified and the terrible consequences of non-submission became ever clearer and ever nearer, Bland's pamphlet stiffened both Virginians' conviction of the justice of their cause and their willingness to go to extremities to assert it. Jefferson later asserted that Bland's pamphlet was the first shot of the Revolution.

We should remember that Richard Bland was Peyton Randolph's first cousin and close friend. What their private conversations covered over the years, we can only imagine.

7

The Death of Speaker
John Robinson and
Randolph's Election as Speaker

1766

John Robinson had held the offices of both Speaker and Treasurer for almost thirty years. He was unquestionably the most powerful man in Virginia and had long been such.

When the issuance of paper money had been authorized during the war, it was legal tender for payments to Virginia at face value. Upon receipt into the Treasury of paper money, the Treasurer was to burn the paper and thus retire the paper currency, which was a form of debt owed by the Colony to its holders. Rumors began to circulate in late 1764 that paper money had been found in circulation that was supposed to have been burned. Richard Henry Lee, an opponent of the Robinson group due to competing land speculations among other reasons, was the primary driver for an audit of the Treasury's books. After an unusually contentious debate, in December 1764, his resolution for an audit was passed by the Burgesses. The committee appointed included Lee, Bland, Harrison, Cary, Burwell, and Dudley Digges. The committee's work was delayed by Robinson.[1]

In May 1765, Pendleton led a bill to borrow £240,000 from London merchant creditors, using £100,000 to call in old paper and replace it with paper currency based on gold. The other £140,000 would be used to create a Loan Office to lend at 5 percent interest on satisfactory security. Lee led a vehement and noisy opposition, saying that the taxes to pay interest on the loan would be paid by another levy on tobacco and that the Loan Office would allow the extravagant and indolent to postpone payment of their debts by borrowing to pay off their existing debts. The bill passed the House anyway, but the odor against it raised by Lee had become so great that the Council killed it.[2]

Robinson had died on May 11, 1766, eight days after news of the Stamp Act's repeal had arrived. He named Peyton Randolph, Pendleton, Peter Randolph, and Lyons as executors. Peyton Randolph hoped to be the new Speaker and Treasurer and declined to serve, due to the conflict of interest. Within a week after Robinson's death, rumors spread of loans made to his friends. The probate court set bond at £250,000. Sureties were Cary, Lewis Burwell, Carter Braxton, Richard Randolph, William Fitzhugh, Charles Carter, John Snelson, and Philip Claiborne.[3]

Governor Fauquier and Pendleton wanted Randolph to be both Speaker and Treasurer. Richard Bland, Lee, and Robert Carter Nicholas wanted the offices of Speaker and Treasurer separated. Fauquier appointed Nicholas as interim Treasurer.[4]

By mid-summer 1766, it was known that Robinson had lent to his friends the paper money turned in to him as Treasurer, which was to have been burned. The executors initially estimated the amount owed to the Colony at £50,000, but the executors did not disclose the names of the debtors of the Robinson Estate, to whom he had lent the money.[5]

The General Assembly convened on November 1, 1766, for the first time since May 31, 1765. Lee ran for Speaker against Randolph, but his support dwindled as George Mercer disclosed that Lee had initially applied for the position of Stamp Agent for himself. Lee's bill to split the offices of Speaker and Treasurer fared better. It passed, paying the Speaker £500 annually. Lee nominated Richard Bland for Speaker. Archibald Cary nominated Randolph, and Randolph was elected. Lee then ran for Treasurer, but the House elected Robert Carter Nicholas as permanent Treasurer, his having served in that interim capacity by appointment of Governor Fauquier.[6]

Randolph's first appointments were for a committee to count votes for doorkeeper: Bland, Lee, Pendleton, Henry, and Wythe.[7] He next appointed the committee to investigate the Treasury, naming a number of the younger members along with the more experienced ones, namely: Bland as chairman, Richard Henry Lee, Wythe, Henry, Cary, John Blair, Jr., Landon Carter, Frank Lee, Thomas Tabb and, from Piedmont, John Fleming and Paul Carrington. Because the executors had not yet disclosed the names of Robinson's debtors, Randolph did not know at the time of the appointments who the debtors were.[8]

When the Treasurer's books were opened, the committee soon learned that the total debt of Robinson's Estate to Virginia was over £100,000, an astounding sum. It was found that his debtors included both executors, three of the estate's sureties, five of the six probate judges, twenty Tidewater Burgesses, and half the Council. The politically prominent debtors included William Byrd III, £10,166; Carter Braxton, £3,469; Charles Carter, Jr., £2,448; Archibald Cary, £3,457; Lewis Burwell, £6,274; John Mercer, £2,713; Edmund Pendleton, £1,020; and John Randolph, £996.[9] Peyton Randolph owed Robinson a few pounds, and Robinson owed him more than that.[10] This information was extracted from Robinson's books with the greatest difficulty, due to great disarray in his records, and was revised from time to time. The shock to the political system was profound, as the General Assembly wrestled with the consequences of discovering that such a large amount of paper money that supposedly had been burned, was in fact still in circulation. Leading members were embarrassed both personally and financially by the disclosures, even though they may not have known the sources of funds that Robinson lent to them. Virginia's credit was at risk, as was the value of its paper. Relations with Great Britain had fortunately been brought to a resting place just before the colony's attention was diverted by these unpleasant matters.

The fact that it was soon apparent that the new Speaker was not tarred by any financial misconduct, despite his being so close to Robinson, could only have enhanced his own position.

8

____

The Speaker Changes Course

Governor Botetourt Opens the General Assembly: May 8, 1769

After an election for a new House of Burgesses, called by the Governor to assemble on a day set by him, the protocol was for the House to assemble and elect their Speaker. The entire House, led by the Speaker-elect, went upstairs in the Capitol to the Council Chamber to call upon the Governor to approve their selection of a Speaker. Upon the Governor's granting his consent, the Speaker then addressed the Governor and "petitioned" him that the House "might enjoy all their ancient Rights and Privileges," including freedom of speech and debate and exemption from arrest, whereupon, the Governor, on behalf of the Crown, would graciously assent.[1]

Norbonne Berkeley, Baron de Botetourt, arrived in October 1768 in time to open the fall 1768 session of the General Court. He later called for election of a new House, to assemble on May 8, 1769. All opening events ran as normal until the Speaker, Peyton Randolph, addressed the Governor. Instead of "petitioning" that the House "might enjoy" its ancient rights and privileges, the Speaker said that the House "lay claim to all its ancient Rights and Privileges."[2]

It is doubtful whether the Governor was aware of the change in form at the time it happened. Experienced Burgesses who had gone through the ceremony several times undoubtedly noticed the change. They would have commented on it to the newer members and word eventually would have reached the Governor's ears, too late to react to it in a timely fashion. It is not likely that Randolph told anyone in advance of what he intended to do, lest the secret reach the Governor

60

Council Chamber, Capitol, Williamsburg (Colonial Williamsburg Foundation, No. T1998-136).

before the ceremony and provoke a controversy with him at the commencement of the session.

It is certain that a careful lawyer like Randolph changed the formula for a reason. And that change indicates a fundamental change in his thinking since May 30, 1765, when he stormed out of the House after its passage of Henry's resolutions. What had brought about his change of mind?

The Townshend Acts: 1767

In 1765, Parliament had passed a Quartering Act in response to colonial opposition to the Stamp Act.[3] For the first time in the colonies, troops could be quartered upon the civilian government, which had

Governor Norborne Berkeley, Baron de Botetourt, engraved by H. Ashby, London, sepia stipple engraving, 1774 (Colonial Williamsburg Foundation, No. DS1999-0120).

to pay for their lodging, fire, candles, salt, vinegar, bedding, cooking utensils, and either cider or beer. General Gage was commander of troops in North America who were stationed in the frontier garrisons and their New York headquarters. Gage quartered troops on the Colony of New York. In June 1766, the New York Assembly refused to provide part of the supplies, contending they were not customary and were a tax. Thus far, there was little or no controversy in Virginia regarding this Act, because no troops were stationed in the colony, and it had no major ports to serve as supply points. On July 2, 1767, the New York Restraining Act suspended the New York Assembly until it complied with Gage's demands. Heretofore, only a Royal Governor could convene or dissolve a colonial Assembly. Now Parliament claimed the right to do so.[4] New York acceded to the demand.

A Townshend Act, passed on June 29, 1767, taxed paper, lead, paint, glass, and tea in the colonies.[5] Thus, Parliament acted to effectuate the Declaratory Act of March 1766, asserting its right to legislate for the colonies in all cases whatsoever. The Act was to be effective on November 20, 1767.

A companion act created a Board of Customs Commissioners and gave colonial courts power to issue general writs of assistance, frequently called general warrants, allowing searches for smuggled contraband.[6] Such writs of assistance need not describe the object of the search nor the particular place to be searched, but rather allowed the customs officer and his men to search homes, warehouses, or other buildings to see what they could find to seize and to incriminate the owner. The officers filled in the writ of assistance themselves to describe what they had done and found, retroactively justifying their search and seizure of goods. This practice eventually gave rise to the prohibition against such searches and seizures in our Bill of Rights. The Virginia courts did not approve a general writ and would issue special writs only, requiring that the place to be searched and the object of the search be identified.

Still another Townshend Act appropriated £40,000 a year to pay military expenses in North America, payable from the revenues being raised, including full implementation of the Proclamation of 1763, ejecting settlers from lands west of the Alleghenies or even east of the mountains where no Indian grant could be shown. The appropriation also was to pay the salaries of royal officers in the colonies who had previously been paid by the colonial Assemblies, thus freeing the royal officers from potential influence by the colonials.[7]

Townshend told the Commons in 1767 that he "would 'in time' do everything to form a revenue to bear the whole but included by degrees and with great delicacy."[8] These Townshend Acts, considered together, manifested the Ministry's clear intent to subjugate the colonies. They asserted the right to levy internal taxes, to free royal officials from colonial influence, to enforce the Proclamation Line of 1763, to enforce the previous acts regulating and taxing commerce, even with general writs of assistance, to use military force where required, and to suppress colonial Assemblies at will.

John Dickinson's Letters from "A Farmer"

Initially, not much attention was given to the Townshend duties. They were payable by the importer, who passed on his costs to the customer, but they were not noticeable by the buyer. This inattention was halted, and vehement protests commenced due to the efforts of John Dickinson. Dickinson, a Pennsylvania lawyer and former member of its Assembly, published a series of twelve Letters from "A Farmer" during the period December 2, 1767–February 15, 1768. They were picked up and eventually reprinted in whole or in part in 20 of the 26 newspapers in the colonies.

Until this time, most colonials, even in Virginia, had acknowledged Britain's right to impose duties for the purpose of regulating commerce, such as preventing importation from countries other than Britain, and also the right of Britain to levy external taxes, such as duties on imports and exports. Dickinson effectively disputed both of these distinctions. Dickinson pointed to Britain's increasingly exercised power to prohibit colonial purchases from any place but Britain and sales to any place other than Britain. Britain had also prohibited many types of manufacturing that would place colonial manufacturers in competition with British manufacturers. If, in addition to these powers, Britain had the right to impose taxes on goods that the colonies could import only from Britain, it could milk the colonies and turn them into "abject slaves."

The tenth letter pointed to Ireland as a timely object lesson of what might be expected to befall the colonists if they should submit to the yoke of British taxation. Following the establishment of a permanent revenue for the Crown in Ireland, the revenue had been applied not chiefly to the benefit of the people of that nation, but to the support of a horde of British pensioners and holders of sinecure offices. To the extent of around £15,000 a year—the private revenue of the King—the pensions were not subject to criticism, but they had long far exceeded that amount and, in two recent years alone, had been increased by more than £158,000. "Besides the burdens of *pensions* in Ireland," Dickinson pointed out, "almost all the *offices* in that poor kingdom have been bestowed upon strangers…. In the same manner shall we unquestionably be treated, as soon as the late taxes levied upon us shall make posts in the 'government' and the 'administration of justice' [quoting the Townshend Act] *here* worth the attention of people of influence in *Great Britain.*"[9]

General Assembly, March 31, 1768: Protest and Petitions

Governor Fauquier died on March 3, 1768. The President of the Council, John Blair, Sr., the leading member of Blair, Russell & Co., became Acting Governor, and decided to allow the late Governor's previous call for the General Assembly to go forward.

The General Assembly convened on March 31, 1768. Randolph, as Speaker, had received the Massachusetts House's February 11, 1768, circular letter to all Speakers, notifying them of their protest to the King of taxation without representation and requesting other colonies to join them. Their letter was laid on the table for study and then referred to the Committee of the Whole, along with resolutions from Virginia's counties regarding the Townshend Acts.[10]

The Burgesses on April 7 approved a Petition to the King, a Memorial to the Lords, and a Remonstrance to the Commons. Randolph appointed Richard Bland, Treasurer Robert Carter Nicholas, Edmund Pendleton, Archibald Cary, John Woodbridge, John Blair, Jr., Dudley Digges, John Page, Severn Eyre, Frank Lee, Benjamin Harrison, and John Alexander to draft the resolutions.[11] Since Randolph was still pursuing the time-tested method of petition and remonstrance, note that the leaders of the radicals were not included, although several new or younger men were, along with a handful of radical rank and file. The House then passed the addresses, asserting that Parliament had no power of internal taxation and police powers in the colonies. Only colonial legislatures had such power, acting with the consent of the

Crown. They pointed out the danger of the suppression of the New York Assembly; if Parliament could order New York to supply General Gage with one item, it could order supply of all items. Finally, they requested repeal of these Acts, pointing out the colonists' alternative not to import and to live on their own. Unlike the House's response to the Stamp Act, this time they were united. The Petition, Memorial, and Remonstrance were adopted unanimously.[12] The Council concurred with the House and instructed the London agent for the Governor and Council to join with the General Assembly's agent in advocacy in London.[13]

All Burgesses and Councilors were now committed to the position that Parliament's acts were unconstitutional. In the Stamp Act debates, several Members had conceded Parliament's right to legislate on the colonies' internal affairs, and Henry's resolutions were opposed by almost half the members voting. Randolph, knowing that his committee would dispute Parliament's power, included a few radicals on the committee to test their willingness to pursue the moderate course of petition to gain their point on the constitutionality of Parliament's action, and he correctly foresaw their choice. He thereby achieved unanimity. Other than unanimity, no new ground of consequence was opened by these petitions. They were explicit but temperate. What was new was that the Speaker was instructed to notify Massachusetts that "Virginia could not but applaud them in their attention to American liberty" and to inform all colonies of Virginia's action and its belief that all colonies should unite in opposition.

Transportation and Extra-Constitutional Convention in Massachusetts

Before the General Assembly convened again, the situation deteriorated further. On June 30, 1768, the Governor of Massachusetts dissolved the Massachusetts House for its refusal to rescind its February 11 circular letter to the other colonies.[14] In July 1768, the Crown's Ministry proposed that colonials charged with treason should be transported to Britain for trial, pursuant to long-disused Acts of Henry VIII.

In August 1768, the Massachusetts merchants declared a boycott of trade with Britain, effective November 1, 1769, thus allowing more than a year for pressure on British merchants to bring about repeal. They were followed by merchants in Salem, Massachusetts, and in New York. On September 22, 1768, representatives of many Massachusetts towns and counties met in a Convention and requested support from other colonies. Massachusetts thereby led the way in organizing revolutionary Conventions to replace the constitutional governments suppressed by Britain. On October 1, 1768, British troops disembarked at Boston.[15] This action had obviously been ordered even before the boycott declaration in August, due to slowness of communication of reports to Britain and organization of an expeditionary force and its transportation to Boston. Hoping to transport the Massachusetts leaders, the British Attorney General and Solicitor General searched the record of the September 1768 Convention and reluctantly held there was insufficient evidence of treason to arrest them.

Arrival of Governor Botetourt

Norborne Berkeley, Baron de Botetourt, arrived in Williamsburg in October 1768, shortly before the convening of the General Court. The Virginians were flattered that a baron had been sent as their Governor, rather than having the titular Governor in Britain and a lower-ranking official serving as Lieutenant Governor on half of the Governor's salary, provided by the taxpayers of Virginia. Lord Jeffrey Amherst unsuccessfully raised a ruckus in London over the loss of his £3,000 annual sinecure. Lord Botetourt impressed the Virginians with the majesty of his equipage. Among these were a coach given to him by the King's uncle, the Duke of Cumberland, drawn by six matched cream-white horses with silver-mounted harness. Such a coach had never been seen in Virginia before. (After Botetourt's death in October 1770, Washington announced his arrival in the ranks of the richest Virginians by buying the Botetourt horses and harness.) Botetourt made a favorable impression and became well-liked during his entire period as Governor. Furthermore, he was well-impressed by Virginia's leading citizens, who appeared in Williamsburg from all over the colony for the General Court. They wined and dined him to their best ability. He learned rapidly that the Virginians were determined not to yield on the constitutional issues.[16]

The King's Speech from the Throne: November 8, 1768

Upon the opening of a newly elected Parliament, the King gave his Speech from the Throne on November 8, 1768. He declared that Massachusetts was in "a state of disobedience to all law and government" and "in a disposition to throw off their dependence upon Great Britain." He asked Parliament to punish the offenders. The Governor of Massachusetts was instructed to submit a list of the principal offenders and information on all treasons committed within the last year "in order that his Majesty may issue a special commission for inquiring of, hearing and determining the said offenses within this realm," pursuant to the Acts of Henry VIII, which criminalized actions outside England as well as within it. Those were the only Acts found which would allow trial in Britain for offenses in the colonies, and the only crime covered was treason. Parliament endorsed the King's proposal that same month. The Lords addressed the King, asking him to secure information on treason in Massachusetts and to bring the offenders to England for trial under the statutes of Henry VIII. The Commons concurred.[17]

The intent behind the Ministry's dissolution of the Massachusetts Assembly and the purpose of sending troops to Boston became crystal clear when considered in the light of the King's Speech. The unmistakable intent was to use whatever force was required to suppress the ferment in Massachusetts. Beyond that, the Crown's intent was also applicable to the leaders of any other colony who objected to subjugation and being reduced to a source of pillage for the King's and Ministry's friends. Randolph did not miss the point. Nor did other leaders in Virginia. Richard Henry Lee concluded that the Townshend Acts were "a flaming sword pointed at liberties."[18] Washington wrote to George Mason on April 5, 1769, enclosing a copy of the Philadelphia non-importation agreement of February 6, 1769: "At a time when our lordly Masters in Great Britain will be satisfied with nothing less than the depreciation of American freedom, it seems highly necessary that something be done to avert the stroke and maintain the liberty which we had derived from our ancestors; but the manner of doing it to answer the purpose effectively is the point in question. That no man should scruple, or hesitate a moment to use a_ms in defense of so valuable a blessing ... is clearly my opinion; yet a_ms should be the last resort.... Addresses to the Throne and remonstrances to Parliament we have already, it is said, proved the inefficacy of; how far their attention to our rights and privileges is to be awakened or alarmed by starving their trade and manufactures, remains to be tried."[19]

The British Context—John Wilkes

John Wilkes won a lawsuit in 1766 that held that general warrants were unlawful in Britain. Subsequently, in March 1768, Wilkes won election as Member of Parliament for Middlesex County (London). The House of Commons refused to seat him.[20] William Lee, one of the Lee brothers, the first American to be elected Alderman in London, and his brother, Arthur Lee, had supported Wilkes.[21] Note that the Townshend Acts, passed in June–July 1767, authorized the issuance of writs of assistance for America, a practice which had just been held unlawful in Britain. It is easy to see how the colonists came to feel a kinship to Wilkes and that his cause was their own, and vice versa.

Wilkes was again elected to Parliament in October 1768, and Parliament again refused to seat him. This action led many Americans to believe that Parliament was not acting in error, but rather was one with the Ministry in trampling upon rights both in Britain and in the colonies.[22] All these events in Britain appeared related to similar actions in the colonies and, by March 1769, enabled many in the colonies to become convinced—correctly, as shown by the description of secret policy toward the colonies in the communication of the Board of Trade to the Privy Council previously quoted—that Britain's goal was to subjugate and loot the colonies. After the King's November 8, 1768, Speech to Parliament, it was no longer realistic to believe that a good King was being misled by bad advisors. Certainly Randolph no longer had any illusions or doubts regarding Britain's policy, as his actions demonstrate from this point forward.

8. The Speaker Changes Course

General Assembly, May 8, 1769: Defiance and Dissolution

A newly elected House of Burgesses convened on May 8, 1769. In the opening ceremonies, Randolph had unilaterally changed the basis of the House's claim to legitimacy, as we have seen. The House would no longer act by the Crown's gracious consent but rather as of right. The change was momentous.

On May 8, 1769, after Randolph had "laid claim" to the House's rights when the session opened, he informed the House that he had complied with their instruction at the last session to write Speakers of the other colonies. He had received several replies. These were laid on the table for examination, along with correspondence with the General Assembly's London agent and correspondence of the Committee of Correspondence. He also notified the House that three treason statutes had been revived in Britain to allow colonials to be tried for treason in England, and those statutes were laid on the table. The rest of the week the House handled the most pressing of its routine matters to avoid arousing the Governor's suspicion.

It was not until May 16 that the House resolved itself into a Committee of the Whole in order "to consider the present state of the colony," referring to an innocuous passage in the Governor's address. The three English statutes on treason were referred to the Committee. The Committee of the Whole then went into secret session. Late in the day, four resolutions were reported to the House: (1) The sole right of taxing Virginia "is now and ever hath been legally and constitutionally vested in the House of Burgesses." (2) Virginians have the undoubted right to petition their Sovereign for redress of grievances and to solicit support of other English colonies. (3) Trials for treason or any felony or crime committed in Virginia "ought of right" to be tried in the colony where it was committed, and seizing colonials and transporting them for trial outside the colony "is highly derogatory of the rights of British subjects." (4) The Burgesses authorized an address to the King to petition for removal of these threats to liberty. All four resolutions of the Committee of the Whole were then approved by the House without dissent. Randolph appointed a committee to draft the address to the

King. John Blair, Jr., was chairman, and the other members were Henry, Richard Henry Lee, Thomas Mason, Nicholas, and Harrison. Overnight, an address to the King was prepared. The House adopted the resolution approving the Address to the King without a dissenting voice. They further resolved that copies be sent to all other Speakers with a request that they concur. The House ordered the Resolves to be printed.[23] Note that the first Resolve directly challenged and denied the powers claimed by Parliament in the Declaratory Act of 1766 and the Townshend Act levying internal taxes on the colonies in 1767. The second Resolve directly challenged and denied the assertion by the Crown in Boston that the leaders of Massachusetts had acted contrary to law in asking other colonies to support them. The third Resolve specifically challenged and denied the right of the King, asserted to Parliament on November 8, 1768, and of Parliament in granting him the powers requested, to transport a colonial leader to Britain for trial by a court in Britain for alleged treason in actions taken by him in the colony. Under Randolph's leadership, the House had unanimously taken on the King, Ministry, and Parliament in unequivocal terms.

After the House came out of secret session, a messenger from the Governor was admitted, summoning the House to the Council Chamber. Randolph led the way. Governor Botetourt sat alone at the Council table. "I have heard of your Resolves and auger ill of their effect." He thereupon dissolved the House.[24]

Formation of the Association: May 17, 1769

The Burgesses had anticipated dissolution, so it was no surprise. They had acted in secret session, so they could not be dissolved before their work was done. Now, word was passed to gather at Raleigh's Tavern, which had the largest non-governmental meeting room in Williamsburg. Most of the Burgesses assembled in the Apollo Room in the afternoon of May 17, 1769.

Randolph was elected "Moderator" of the meeting. It was apparent that the Burgesses were now ready to restrict importation of British goods into Virginia. Washington pulled a draft of Articles of Associ-

8. The Speaker Changes Course

72

ation from his pocket, the only member so prepared. He and his neighbor, George Mason of Gunston Hall, had discussed the shape of a non-importation association, and Washington had sent Mason a copy of Philadelphia's recently adopted non-importation agreement. Mason drafted Articles, and Washington presented them and spoke to them. Randolph appointed a committee to draft the Articles of Association, which included Washington, Henry, and Lee.[25]

The committee reported a draft on May 18. The Articles first asserted loyalty to the Crown but declared the revenue portion of the Townshend Acts unconstitutional and called on British merchants to obtain repeal. The signers agreed to import and to buy none of the articles taxed by the Townshend Acts after September 1, 1769, except cheap paper. In addition, they agreed not to import a long list of other goods, including slaves. Allowed items included cloth for slaves, spices, and sewing needles. Prohibited items included all luxuries of food and dress, alcohol, and almost all manufactured goods. If not repealed, tobacco exports would be stopped the following year in order to damage the Crown's revenues. The Stamp Act Associations did not purport to act on anyone but their members, but these Articles were intended to operate on everyone in the colony. The local committee were to call on merchants who imported prohibited goods and request that they be returned. If a merchant refused, his conduct would be published. Enforcement was to be by example, persuasion, and ostracism of those not complying.[26]

On May 18, 1769, the Associators approved and signed the Articles of Association. Of 116 Burgesses, 88 signed as Associators on that day.[27] A number had gone home before the Townshend Act had been taken up. Randolph signed at the top of the first column and Patrick Henry at the top of the other column. Within two months, George Wythe published the names of eleven more Members who had signed, a total of 99 out 116.[28] Benjamin Harrison and John Randolph, Peyton's brother and brother-in-law, declined to sign.

Opposite top: Raleigh Tavern, exterior (Colonial Williamsburg Foundation, No. D2014-DMD-1029-4468). *Bottom: Apollo Room, Raleigh Tavern, Williamsburg* (Colonial Williamsburg Foundation, No. T1980-395).

A Change in Virginia's Political Climate

At the time the "Associators" acted, they knew of other non-importation agreements in Boston, Providence, Newport, New York, and Philadelphia, a list of all major ports north of Virginia except Annapolis.[29] The Northern colonies were generally faster in answering the call of the Massachusetts Assembly for non-importation in February 1768 and its call for a boycott in August 1768. However, the non-importation agreements of all the other colonies were only agreements among the merchants of the principal ports, and the scope of the Virginia Association was much broader and more drastic than any non-importation agreements adopted elsewhere. Most importantly, the Virginia Association was the act of the Burgesses of Virginia, representing the entire colony and its political leadership. Finally, unlike the other agreements, the Virginia Associators'

Top: George Washington as Colonel in the Virginia Regiment, **Charles Willson Peale, oil on canvas, 1772. (No. U1897.1.1, Gift of George Washington Custis Lee, Washington & Lee University, Lexington, Virginia).** *Bottom: George Mason, a 19th century* **copy in oil on canvas by Louis Mathieu Didier Guillaume (1816–1892) of a lost portrait by John Hesselius (1728–1778), painted before 1778 (Virginia Historical Society, No. 1858.2).**

announced intention was to act upon the entire population of Virginia, rather than just the Associators.[30] Virginia's response was the most radical, even though the Townshend Act had less effect in Virginia than in the North.[31] In Virginia, the Northern Neck planters, Washington, Lee, and Mason, were among the most forward of the leaders for non-importation.[32] As of May 1769, the Virginians were not aware that the Ministry, having ordered dissolution of the Massachusetts Assembly on April 21, 1768, had also ordered all colonial Governors to dissolve any colonial legislature that endorsed Massachusetts' actions.[33] While not having been notified of the Ministry's intent, the Virginians had surmised as much from the tone of the Ministry's public actions and the King's November Speech, so they had forestalled the Burgesses' dissolution by a secret session. That the House had acted nevertheless without dissent in its support for Massachusetts shows how far the Virginians' thinking had changed since the Stamp Act days.

One must conclude that, at the time the Burgesses convened on May 8, 1769, Randolph had already ascertained the Burgesses' state of mind, anticipated the Governor's reaction, and determined upon his own leadership of extra-constitutional resistance upon dissolution. His change in phrasing the House's allegiance to the Crown—abandoning the traditional petition for the Crown's grant of rights to a claim of those rights—indicates that he anticipated the event and had settled his mind as to his own course of action. On May 16, Randolph had appointed three radicals, including their leaders, Henry and Richard Henry Lee, to a six-man House committee to draft a Petition to the King. The three conservatives included John Blair, Jr., as chairman, whose father was the principal in the land company that had blocked the Ohio Company of Richard Henry Lee in 1753–1754. Harrison had been a principal in the Loyal Company and was presently an investor in the new Grand Ohio Company, which was still contesting western speculations with the predominantly Northern Neck investors. Lee had led the investigation into Speaker John Robinson's misuse of the colony's money and greatly damaged many of the friends of the conservative members of the committee, who themselves had not owed Robinson money and were not personally caught up in the scandal. These men—Harrison, Blair, and Nicholas—covered the range of conservative thought; Harrison did not sign the Articles of Association two days later. With no tie-breaking member on the committee, we must conclude that Randolph deliberately created a committee made up of men that he knew all opposed the encroachment on Virginia's rights, with a view to giving them the opportunity for the first time to work together and come to an agreement. Randolph, as Moderator of the Association, appointed Henry, Lee, and Washington to draft the Articles of Association. We do not have the names of any appointees of a more moderate approach, and there probably were none. Randolph had obviously concluded that determined action was necessary, as there now existed unity of purpose, and appointed a committee that would give him what he wanted.

Randolph had clearly changed his approach between the March 1768 and May 1769 sessions of the General Assembly. We must remember that Randolph had better information regarding events in Britain than any other man in Virginia, so we must take into consideration the events in Britain as well as those in the various colonies, allowing for a time lag of several weeks due to slow and irregularly scheduled shipping.

During the year between these two sessions of the General Assembly, Randolph learned that the Ministry was willing to use troops against the people of London and order the troops to fire upon them. He also knew that troops had disembarked in Boston on October 1, 1768, and he could have had no doubt that the Ministry were willing to use them against colonials, if they were willing to use them in London itself. Wilkes was again elected to Parliament in February 1769, but Parliament voted to expel him. By this time, the efforts of the King and the Ministry to control Parliament had borne fruit. On the Government (Tory) bench, 192 out of 262 Members of Parliament held Crown offices.[34] Tory government had reduced the concept of an independent Parliament to a legal fiction. Randolph had also known since late summer 1768 that the Ministry had sought, and then obtained, the right to transport colonial leaders to Britain to stand trial for treason.

The King's Speech, news of which could not have reached Virginia until at least December 1768, was the critical event. The King's unnecessarily inflammatory language showed his personal determination to subjugate all the colonies. Any leaders opposing Britain would be arrested, transported to Britain for trial, and executed. Randolph was among their number.

Transportation to Britain for trial was not just an inconvenience. It meant the defendants would be separated by 3,000 miles and a lengthy, expensive, and dangerous ocean voyage from their families, friends, and properties that might support a defense and might alleviate the miseries of an eighteenth-century prison. Defense witnesses would need to be brought to Britain and maintained there for months or years while awaiting trial, at least some of them at the defendants' expense. The trial venue and makeup of the jury panel would be subject to manipulation by the Crown's attorneys in order to assure a forum hostile to defendants.

What was the only crime that would allow such transportation for trial? Treason. The latest rebels to commit treason against the Crown were the Jacobites, who supported Bonnie Prince Charlie's Stuart rising in 1745–1746. What was the punishment that might await such a traitor? The last Jacobite to be executed, only twenty years previously, was the Scottish Lord Lovat, who was sentenced to be hanged, drawn, and quartered. We know today that Lord Lovat was the last man to have been condemned to these horrors, but no colonial leader in 1769 could have known that!

Colonials who resisted would be fired upon and brought to heel. Parliament's rejection of London's election of Wilkes in the October election emphasized Parliament's fixed determination to put down resistance even in the capital, and even more assuredly by despised colonials. A newly elected Parliament, its Ministry, and the King had chosen a common path—the subjugation of resistance at home and abroad. Randolph, from this point forward, was never provided with new facts that would change the conclusion he had reached during the critical months, December 1768–May 1769. As Speaker, it was his prerogative to appoint the committees.[35] Randolph's appointment of Henry, Lee, and one other radical to a six-man drafting committee during the secret session of the House on May 16, together with the appointments of radicals that he made as Moderator of the Association, publicly brought the radicals into Virginia's "government" in May 1769.

Randolph's every action from May 1769 forward reflects his unexpressed conclusion that the only safety for Virginia and for himself personally was dependent on some sort of separation from the government of Great Britain.

Thus far, Randolph had achieved unity of purpose among Virginians in opposing internal taxation and transportation for trial. Only 10 percent of the Burgesses had opposed the Association, because it was clearly extra-constitutional, but 90 percent had been willing to act extra-constitutionally. Randolph's efforts would be directed to restoring virtual unanimity rather than relying on majority rule, whereby those who dissented from the course of opposition chosen by the majority could themselves be subjugated by that majority.

Randolph's First Trip North

In October 1767, Randolph had been appointed to a Commission to settle the boundary between Pennsylvania and New York. The Commission finally met in New York in late summer 1769. On his trip to New York, he stopped several days in Philadelphia and met with many of the local leaders. Upon arriving in New York, where the Commission met, he also took the opportunity to meet the local leaders as well as members of the Commission. This was his first trip north of the Chesapeake region.[36] He undoubtedly discussed with these men in both cities their reaction to the actions of Britain and the colonies' response. He left the Commission before it completed its work, because in August 1769, Governor Botetourt called for new elections on September 9, 1769, for Burgesses and a General Assembly to convene on November 7. He had been again elected Burgess for Williamsburg. Randolph arrived home on September 28. He now had direct experience with some other colonial leaders, and his confidence in their ability was apparently enhanced.

The Non-Importation Association and Partial Repeal of the Townshend Act

The non-importation agreement proved to be complicated in practice. Violations of the agreement were numerous.[37] Efforts were made to reduce Virginia's reliance on imports. Randolph became president of a company formed to build a factory to make cloth.[38]

Efforts to interpret the non-importation agreement were slow to be put into effect. These efforts became less important as rumors and then the fact of repeal became known. It was the effect on British merchants of non-importation in Northern colonies, especially in New England, that brought about a tactical retreat by the Ministry.

In early August, Governor Botetourt received word that the Ministry would ask Parliament to repeal the revenue portion of the Townshend Act.[39] This led him to call for new elections. This information might lead to election of a more moderate House. Botetourt undoubtedly had been concerned by the unanimity of the Burgesses' opposition to the Acts.

When the General Assembly convened, he notified them formally of the Ministry's decision, "upon consideration of such duties having been laid contrary to true principles of commerce,"[40] reserving only the tax on tea. The session was quiet, but all the Virginia ladies wore Virginia cloth to the Christmas Ball at the Governor's Palace. King George III instructed his Governor, upon his appointment, to inform the next Assembly of "our firm resolution to support and preserve entire our antient, just and constitutional Right to enact Laws by and with the consent of our Parliament, to bind all and every part of our Empire in all cases whatsoever, and that We are determined to ... reject as null and void, every Act and proceeding in our Colonies, inconsistent with and derogatory from Our said Rights, and We do therefore highly disapprove their said Petition [from the March 31, 1778, session] to Us."[41] The Governor exercised his own better judgment and did not deliver any part of his instruction to the Virginians. Nevertheless, the King's determination did not auger well for the future.

Lord Frederick North became First Lord of the Treasury and Prime Minister. Debate in the Cabinet centered on the advisability of retaining the tax on tea. On March 1, 1770, the Cabinet voted to retain the tax by a majority of one. On March 5, he asked Parliament to repeal all Townshend duties, except on tea, in order to preserve the principle that Parliament could tax the colonies in absolute right. On March 18, 1770, the revenue provisions were repealed, except for tea. In Parliament, the vote in April 1770 for total repeal was 142, which failed, and for repeal except on tea, 204, a majority.[42] Parliament thereby again asserted its claim to tax the colonies in absolute right.

Second Non-Importation Agreement: June 22, 1770

The May 1770 meeting of the General Assembly was quiet insofar as the Townshend Act went. Members awaited official notice of repeal and what shape it would take. News had been received that troops had fired on townspeople in Boston on March 5, 1770, but the troops responsible had been arrested and were awaiting trial.

While the Burgesses were in town, Randolph called a meeting of the 1769 Associators. Pendleton and Nicholas argued that Parliament had compromised, and that Virginia should accept the tax on tea. Landon Carter disagreed with Pendleton and Nicholas that non-importation should continue and on a broader list than just tea.[43] Randolph appointed a committee of ten, including Washington, to modify the 1769 Articles. They recommended that luxuries and expensive goods should be retained on the list. The new Articles of Agreement on non-importation were adopted on June 22, 1770. The new Articles created five-man committees in each county to attempt enforcement by publishing the violators.[44] In calling the meeting and in choosing his committee, Randolph thereby preserved Virginia's opposition in principle to Parliament's claim of right to lay internal taxes on Virginia.

Lord North had succeeded in his goal to quiet the colonists. The heat had gone out of the tax issue. Most of the Northern colonies resumed importation of all items but tea, a position not nearly as strict as that taken by Virginia.[45] In New York and Philadelphia, the merchants opened tea trade directly with Holland in violation of the Navigation Acts going back to 1653, Cromwell's Commonwealth.[46] Many Virginians became apathetic. After repeal in April 1770, many Virginians even bought taxed tea. Between December 1, 1770, and January 5, 1773, duty was paid in Virginia on 80,000 pounds of tea.[47]

Lord North's publicly stated intent to tax tea in order to preserve the principle of Parliament's right to do so was still remembered. The non-importation of tea was done to preserve the principle of its unconstitutionality, even though non-importation was honored only in the breach by many in Virginia during this period. In Virginia, the meetings of Associators slackened. In July 1771, Washington and Mason wrote Randolph that, in parts of Virginia, importers were ignoring the Association, and the Potomac should do so too, except as to tea. All other colonies had stopped the boycott except as to taxed tea. Randolph's published notices of meetings were followed by announcements that meetings had been postponed due to poor attendance. Governor Botetourt died in October 1770, and his successor, John Murray, Earl of Dunmore, arrived in July 1771. During the July 1771 session, Randolph called a meeting of Associators, and they agreed to limit the boycott to tea. The members felt a desire to wind this down in order to get a fresh start with the new Governor.[48]

9

From the Townshend Acts
to the *Gaspee* Incident,
1768–1772

The End of the Golden Age

Tobacco, the Indian trade, and speculation in Western lands had fueled the successful economy that produced the Virginia dynasties and their great houses. Virginia had flourished despite the Navigation Acts passed during the dictatorship of Oliver Cromwell and expanded under Charles II. These Acts required all tobacco exports to go to Britain and to be carried in British ships.[1] Of the tobacco thus exported to Britain, only 10 percent was consumed in Britain, and 90 percent was re-exported at a profit by merchants in Britain. Virginia, therefore, did not benefit from a "compensating monopoly" of the British tobacco imports. Daniel Dulaney, a Maryland lawyer and planter, estimated that the cost to Maryland and Virginia of this restriction on their tobacco exports amounted to £270,000 a year. In addition, the Crown imposed heavy duties on tobacco imported into Britain.[2] Washington's careful bookkeeping showed that tobacco duties and shipping expenses took 74 percent of his gross sales income from tobacco. Unlike the New Englanders, Virginians did not resort to smuggling to evade these burdens. They did not own large numbers of ships and, even if they had tried, all Virginia shipping passed through a single exit: the strait between Norfolk and Virginia's Eastern Shore of the Chesapeake. Because of his meticulous review of his finances, Washington ceased planting tobacco and switched to wheat, which he could legally sell to British possessions in the West Indies. The profitability of tobacco has

82

probably been overemphasized, and the importance of the other sources of income underemphasized because Virginia prospered greatly until the 1750s.

The expense of the French and Indian War, starting in 1754, burdened the colony's finances. It issued paper money for the first time in 1755, the last colony to do so.[3] In 1757, a severe drought caused such a reduction in the tobacco production that the price rose to 50 shillings (50/-) per cwt. (per hundred pounds). A 1758 Act of the General Assembly allowed debts denominated in pounds of tobacco to be paid in currency at 2d (two pence) per pound (or 16/8d, sixteen shillings, eight pence, per cwt.). This temporary measure was disallowed by the Ministry two years later. It gave rise to the Parson's Case, a suit by clergy to enforce their right to payment in tobacco, in which Patrick Henry first gained prominence by representing a vestry against their parson in December 1763.

The 1759 crop sold at prices up to 35/- per cwt. The British merchants, whose agents in Virginia bought most of the colony's tobacco, began to agree among themselves regarding the maximum price they would pay.[4] Many of the major merchants in Virginia were Scots out of Glasgow after they were allowed access to English colonies under the Act of Union in 1707. They refused to hire Virginians to work in their businesses because they regarded Virginians as too easy on extending credit and not tough enough in collecting debts. The Scots were widely hated.[5] The high prices of 1758–1760 were the last hurrah for tobacco. By 1761, the price had declined to 16/8d. The "foreign" (Scottish and English) merchants used the emergency price set by the 1758 Act as a cap for the price of tobacco. Through the 1760s, the price of tobacco was in a general decline despite the reopening of the French and Spanish markets when the War ended in 1763.[6] In 1763, tobacco fell to a new low of 12/6d. Many planters had two years' inventory on hand and finally had to sell for what they could get.[7] In 1764, the Scots bought tobacco in Virginia at 12/6d. Prices continued to be depressed throughout the 1760s.[8] In August 1769, the worst hurricane in living memory hit Virginia. Crops, warehouses, docks, homes, and other improvements from the Potomac to the James were destroyed, along with much loss of life of people and livestock.[9] That year, the merchants debated among themselves whether to drive the price to 16/- or 18/- and finally agreed among themselves on 16/8d again. Even many large planters could no longer draw on their accounts in London to be paid from next year's crop as had been their practice.[10] In the spring of 1771, there was a great flood on the Rappahannock, the James, and the Roanoke Rivers that destroyed the 1770 tobacco crop in the warehouses, as well as fences, livestock, soil, houses, and lives. The disaster was of such an unprecedented nature that a special session of the General Assembly was called in order to give relief for the loss of tobacco. In 1773, the price of tobacco had been driven down to 14/-, and in June 1774 it was even lower, 12/6d.[11] The constantly fluctuating price of tobacco, with a declining trend, created constant economic uncertainty.[12]

Against this backdrop of economic decline, let us look again at the actions of the British government. The war had begun with Virginia's effort to secure the forks of the Ohio River in 1754. This strategic point was necessary to secure Virginia's claims in the Ohio Valley and the right to make land grants, populate it, and control the trade with the Indians in the Ohio Valley. Braddock failed in the 1755 attempt, which cost him and many others their lives. British troops thereafter made no further attempt, operating from Virginia. Lee and Washington were both convinced that the British commander in the area, General Forbes, postponed action against Fort Duquesne in order to promote the interests of the British Superintendent of Northern Indian Affairs, Sir William Johnson, the Philadelphia merchants, and the Loyal Company.[13] By 1758, pressure on Canada led the French to abandon Fort Duquesne. British troops built a road to Fort Pitt from Fort Carlisle in Pennsylvania, which gave Philadelphia merchants better access to the Ohio Valley Indians. In 1759, their Indian trade amounted to the great sum of £30,000. The Pennsylvanians remained the sole beneficiaries of this trade until 1774, excluding the Virginia Indian traders, whose business was thereby limited to the Cherokees and other Southern tribes, which were already in decline.[14]

The Proclamation of October 1763, voiding existing land grants west of the Appalachians and excluding all colonials from the area, dealt the Virginians a terrible blow. They were the primary—and strongest—claimants to the Ohio Valley lands. All three of the sources of their prosperity had been injured: namely, tobacco, Indian trade, and speculation in Western lands. Between 1762 and 1764, the value of slaves in Virginia declined 50 percent.[15] The colonies generally suffered a depression in 1764, but Virginia was the hardest hit.[16]

The Currency Act of 1764 shrank the supply of money and credit. Among the landed gentry, the scarcity of money in lieu of specie, and of specie itself, brought on an increase in debt to a single merchant (Norton) from £11,000 in 1760 to £40,000 in 1773, as well as a decline in land values. Planters' total debt in 1775 was estimated by Jefferson at £2,000,000.[17] The Stamp Act followed in 1765–1766, threatening to drain the colonies of the little specie still in circulation and to bring business to a standstill. With only a year's respite, the Townshend Acts renewed the assault on the shuddering economic and political supports of Virginia and the other colonies. The King's Speech from the Throne on November 8, 1768, expressly laid claim to the right and power of "the King in Parliament" to tax the colonies, limited only by their own discretion. We have examined the effect of this Speech on Randolph and, doubtlessly, many of the other men who made the effort to inform themselves. While the constitutional issues were paramount in Virginia, they did not arise in a vacuum. The actions of Britain's King, Parliament, Ministry, and officers reinforced the determination to preserve Virginia's rights.

Attempted Revival of Western Land Speculation

At the November 1768 session of the General Assembly, Governor Botetourt officially informed the General Assembly that the Townshend duties were to be repealed except on tea. Further, the Treaty of Hard Labour with the Cherokees had been executed on October 18, and it was apparent that the Proclamation of 1763 was being modified. Washington had Governor Dinwiddie's February 18, 1754, Proclamation read and placed on the table, pledging 200,000 acres of land grants for militia volunteers. The next day the House approved an address to Governor Botetourt, asking if any grants had been made between the West line of North Carolina and the junction of the Mississippi and

Ohio Rivers. The Governor answered that no grants had been made.[18] A year later, on December 15, 1769, the officers and men of 1754 petitioned the Governor for their land, with surveys made by their surveyor, on the Monongahela, Great Kanawha, and Sandy Creek, south of the Ohio River in present southwestern Pennsylvania and West Virginia. The Council approved 200,000 acres in 20 tracts. The claims were to be presented to Washington by October 10, 1770, for him to certify to the Council.[19] The Governor sent Washington a map showing the location of a proposed grant to the Philadelphia–Walpole Group, the Grand Ohio Company.[20]

The Pennsylvanians contested Virginia's claims to virtually all the Western lands. In April 1768, a Board of Trade report characterized the 1763 Proclamation Line as a temporary expedient, perhaps to lay the groundwork for the Pennsylvania–London coalition that became the Grand Ohio Company.[21] In November 1768, Sir William Johnson, the Superintendent of Northern Indian Affairs, and representatives of New York, Pennsylvania, and New Jersey met with 2,200 Iroquois and other Indians at Fort Stanwyx, now in upstate New York, to clarify borders between the Indians and colonists. Virginia was not represented, and Fort Pitt was effectively in Pennsylvania's hands. The treaty recognized the Ohio River to the Tennessee River as the boundary between whites and Indians, thereby ignoring Virginia's claims north of the river but opening central Kentucky to settlement. At Fort Stanwyx, Samuel and Thomas Wharton of Philadelphia arranged to buy 2,400,000 acres from the Indians. They organized the Grand Ohio Company (also called Walpole Associates) to do so. The Pennsylvania men with the Whartons included Benjamin Franklin, Robert Morris, John Dickinson, and Joseph Galloway. Lord Hillsborough, Secretary for American Affairs and also President of the Board of Trade, rejected the Fort Stanwyx Treaty for the purchase of 2,400,000 acres, citing the Proclamation of 1763. Some of Robinson's former supporters, led by Carter Braxton and Benjamin Harrison, investors in the Loyal Company, were brought into the Grand Ohio Company. They had been badly hurt by Lee's forcing the Robinson audit. Edmund Pendleton represented them. Thomas Walpole, a merchant banker, nephew of the former Prime Minister Robert Walpole, Lord Camden, and other important men in London were also brought into the Grand Ohio Company. They forced Lord Hillsborough out of office.[22]

In November 1769, the Grand Ohio Company then sought approval in London, bypassing Virginia's claims, to pay £10,460 for 30,000,000 acres south of the Ohio River, located in what is now West Virginia and eastern Kentucky. France had a single agent in London who bought all tobacco imported by France and then resold it in France. In 1769, Walpole was appointed as the French agent. The representative of the Ohio Company in London, George Mercer, unsuccessfully attempted to merge it into the Grand Ohio Company, with an under-the-table stock grant to himself. The Grand Ohio Company stood to control the sale of tobacco and most of the Indian trade. Its proposed grant would include the territory previously granted to the Loyal Company, which had been voided by the Proclamation of 1763, some of whose major investors had been brought into the Grand Ohio Company. Its headquarters would be in London and Philadelphia.[23]

Richard Henry Lee, George Mason, Squire Lee, and Washington defended the interests of the Ohio Company, whose voided grants lay north of the Ohio River.[24] In addition to his own share of the 1754 grant as colonel of the regiment, Washington had bought the claims of some other veterans, for a total interest of 24,100 acres. The 1754 bounty lands, all south of the Ohio River in what is now West Virginia and Southwestern Pennsylvania, were shepherded by Washington through the House, Council, survey, and agreed allocation among the officers and men, the final allotments being actually assigned and patents issued in November 1772 and, as to a balance, in October 1773.[25]

In April 1772, the Privy Council ordered all colonial governors to issue no new land grants pending a review of the western lands by the Board of Trade.[26] It was in the correspondence between the Board and the Privy Council that the Board reminded the Privy Council of the decision to limit settlements to those east of the mountains in order to retain control of the colonies' trade and political domination.[27] In August 1772, the Privy Council conditionally approved the Grand Ohio grant.[28] However, on April 4, 1773, a royal proclamation prohibited western grants except to war veterans.[29] The Privy Council reversed itself, and in January 1774, the Board of Trade announced that all sales west of the mountains would be by auction of small tracts only.[30] Many leading Virginians and Pennsylvanians were sorely disappointed. In February 1774, Governor Dunmore received notice of the Board of Trade's decision against new land grants, which also contained a decision to quadruple the price of land sold in smaller parcels from five shillings to one pound for 100 acres.[31] The treaties with the Cherokees and the Iroquois had ceded the Indians' title to the Crown, and the lands in Kentucky, West Virginia, and Southwestern Pennsylvania were now available in smaller tracts.

As the relationship with Britain continued to deteriorate during the late 1760s and early 1770s, Virginia's interests were clearly opposed to the Pennsylvanians' land grab and continued occupation at Fort Pitt and its control of the Ohio Valley Indian trade. Although some of Robinson's former allies may have become financially interested in the Grand Ohio Company, by early 1774, they learned that their interests were frustrated as completely as the interests of the investors in the Ohio Company. Many leading Virginians were stalemated by the actions of the Ministry. But many less powerful Virginians moved west to take up small tracts under the new rules, in addition to those who settled beyond the mountains under 1754 veterans' claims and those who were just "squatters."

As the Revolution approached, let us review the actual results of all the intrigues and maneuverings involving the great land grants and proposed grants. The grants to the Loyal Company and to the Ohio Company had been voided by the Proclamation of 1763. The proposed grants to the Grand Ohio Company had not been made, but many powerful men in London were trying to reverse the Privy Council's January 1774 decision against the Grand Ohio Company. The bounty grants to the veterans of 1754 were organized and moved forward to a successful conclusion due almost entirely to the efforts of Washington, persistently applied from 1768 to 1773. Even if the proposed grant had been made to the Grand Ohio Company at some date subsequent to the issuance of patents to the officers and men of 1754, Washington believed it unlikely that the Grand Ohio Company would be able to contest their titles successfully, especially if the grantee had taken steps to "seat" or occupy his claim prior to any such conflicting grant. Washington and the other veterans of 1754 alone were successful in reducing land to both title and possession. Many important Virginians were deprived by the British government of their normal ability to obtain grants and eventually resell for a speculative profit, which had been such a major element in their income prior to 1763. Furthermore, Virginians had been excluded from the Indian trade of the Ohio Valley by Pennsylvanians with the assistance of British troops stationed at Fort Pitt. The conflict between investors in the Loyal Company and the Ohio Company had been removed by action of the Ministry detrimental to both.

Actions by the Crown in America and Britain: 1769–1772

Lord North and his Ministry sought to quieten the disturbances in the colonies from the time the Ministry decided to back off (except for the tax on tea). This change of policy was generally successful until a mob in Rhode Island burned a particularly obnoxious Customs cutter, the *Gaspee*, in June 1772.

On March 5, 1770, the same day that Lord North moved to repeal most duties, a Boston mob provoked the so-called "Boston massacre," in which endangered troops fired on the mob. John Adams defended the soldiers arrested by civil authorities, and they were acquitted by a trial jury on October 30, 1770.[32] The affair was handled in a manner satisfactory to the Virginians, despite radical propaganda in Boston.

Other than the "Boston massacre," the Ministry enjoyed peace in the colonies until June 1772. However, in London, the Ministry actively suppressed dissent. In February 1769, John Wilkes was again elected to Parliament, and Parliament expelled him. The fourth time he was elected by a majority of 1,145 to 296, but Parliament seated his opponent.[33] In 1770, the Commons sent an officer into the City of London to arrest a printer, in violation of the hard-fought and long-established liberties of the City. The City put the officer in jail, and Parliament responded by sending the Lord Mayor of London to the Tower.[34] If the wealth and power and historical importance of the City of London did not protect its Lord Mayor in defending its liberties against Parliament, no mere colonial leader was safe. During 1769–1770, one-fourth of the voters in England petitioned the King, to no avail.[35] In March 1771, the King responded to the City's petition by laughing at it and was cold to the City's later petitions in May and November 1771. The effect upon informed colonials was important: if he won't hear the City, he won't hear us. Many colonials no longer believed that the King and Parliament were acting in error or upon bad advice in trampling on colonial rights, but rather that the King, the Ministry, and Parliament were of one mind and acted deliberately.[36]

10

The *Gaspee* Incident and Virginia's New Committee of Correspondence

March 12, 1773

On June 9, 1772, the Customs cutter *Gaspee,* commanded by an especially aggressive lieutenant, was boarded by a Rhode Island mob of more than 100 men who shot and wounded its commander, put him and the crew ashore, and burned the ship to the water's edge. The Ministry appointed a Court of Inquiry in September with authority to identify, charge, and arrest defendants to be transported with all witnesses to Britain for trial.[1]

A Court of Inquiry in Rhode Island! The threat in the 1768 King's Speech against the leaders defending the liberties of Massachusetts, backed up by a swiftly enacted Act of Parliament, had now become reality in Rhode Island. And, if the Lord Mayor of London was not safe, neither were the Virginians nor any other colonials. Reality of the ultimate horrors had now arrived.

A Boston Town Meeting authorized a Committee of Correspondence on November 2, 1772, primarily for maintenance of communications with other Massachusetts towns and counties, since their legislature had been dissolved. Before March 12, 1773, the date set to convene the General Assembly, Richard Henry Lee wrote to Samuel Adams, the leader of the Massachusetts radicals, and to John Dickinson, a radical leader in Philadelphia, suggesting inter-colonial committees of correspondence. Before the General Assembly convened, a nucleus of radicals met to prepare the ground. They were Richard

Henry Lee, Patrick Henry, Frank Lee, Thomas Jefferson, and Jefferson's brother-in-law and close friend, Dabney Carr.[2] When the Burgesses convened on March 12, 1773, Dabney Carr offered two resolutions. The first was to establish a new standing Committee of Correspondence, granting it authority to confer with other colonies and inviting other colonies to establish similar committees in order to maintain contact. The Committee duplicated the function of the pre-existing joint Committee of Correspondence of the Burgesses and Council, in contact with the General Assembly's agent in London in order to give him directions and to obtain information regarding actions in Parliament and Ministry affecting the colonies, but it gave the House a London contact independent of the Council.[3] The second resolution was for the Committee to inform "themselves particularly of the principles and authority on which was constituted a Court of Inquiry said to have been lately held in Rhode Island with power to transport persons, accused of offenses committed in America, to places beyond the seas to be tried."[4] Both resolutions quickly passed the House unanimously. Bland and many other conservatives had become convinced of the futility of protests.[5]

An eleven-man committee was approved, to be made up of the Speaker, the six standing committee chairmen, and four others. The eleven members were named in the report of the Committee of the Whole to the House. It is probable that the members were agreed in advance between Randolph and the radicals, though one writer says the radicals had the temerity to name themselves and some, but not all of the committee chairmen in the resolution, giving themselves control. Agreement in advance as to the men and method is much more likely, and certainly neater, indicating Randolph's hand. The chairmen of the standing committees were Robert Carter Nicholas, who was also Treasurer, Richard Bland, Benjamin Harrison, Edmund Pendleton, Richard Henry Lee, and Archibald Cary, five "conservatives" and one "radical." Randolph appointed four more "radicals": Patrick Henry, Thomas Jefferson, Dabney Carr, and Dudley Digges.[6] Thus, Randolph created a committee with five "conservatives," five "radicals," and himself.

On March 13, 1773, the new Committee of Correspondence met.

They designated a Select Committee, members close to Williamsburg, with authority to act during recesses. The Select Committee were Randolph, Robert Carter Nicholas, and Dudley Digges, one "conservative," one "radical" and Randolph. The first task was to request information regarding the *Gaspee* affair from the Speakers of Massachusetts, Connecticut, Rhode Island, and New York. Also on March 13, the full Committee instructed the Select Committee to send all other Speakers copies of a new Virginia statute making it a felony to counterfeit in Virginia the paper money of any other colony, thereby encouraging the use of committees of correspondence for continuous communication. The new Committee of Correspondence thus opened communication directly with the other colonial legislatures, even though Governor Dunmore had already agreed to send copies of the Act to the other Governors. Governor Hutchinson of Massachusetts saw this act as "an avowal of independency, because it could be justified only upon principles of independence."[7]

The Select Committee met on April 6, 1773, to approve drafts of these letters and to write John Norton, a London merchant, to send the Committee regularly the Commons Journal, Acts of Parliament, and proceedings of the Ministry affecting Virginia.[8]

The observation of Governor Hutchinson, a native of Massachusetts and loyal servant of the Crown who had already suffered the destruction of his home in the Crown's service, was correct. The institutionalization of Committees of Correspondence, permanently embedded in the colonial legislatures and in ongoing communication with each other, began the creation of the machinery of revolution. The idea for such an innovation came from Virginia, specifically from Lee, who had explored the possibility with radical leaders of two of the more important colonies. By June 1773, favorable replies for such committees were received from Massachusetts, Rhode Island, Connecticut, New Hampshire, and South Carolina and from all remaining colonies within a year.[9]

The speed with which Carr's two resolutions were whipped through the House and the speed with which the new committee acted on the very next day are sufficient proof that this legislative action had been planned in advance. The "radical" caucus of the two Lees, Henry,

10. *Gaspee* and Virginia's New Committee of Correspondence

Jefferson, and Carr were only one handle of the levers effecting these actions. Of necessity, some representative or representatives of the "radicals," brought by Randolph into the "government" of the colony in 1769 after the King's Speech, conferred with Randolph in the privacy of his home in Williamsburg. The concept of creating a new super-committee as a new standing committee, whose members included the leaders of the House—the Speaker and the chairmen of all the other standing committees—probably came from the fruitful mind and vast experience of Randolph. It was probably also Randolph's suggestion to have the Speaker appoint sufficient additional members, with the intent and understanding that he would appoint enough of the younger radicals, even though they had not yet achieved leadership positions in the House, in order to balance the new committee and to give Randolph the determining vote in the event of any disagreement within the committee. There is no proof as to how this all was put together, but we can be positive that it was put together in advance of March 12, 1773. Lee's concept for intercolonial communication was probably given its structure by Randolph. The result was creation in Virginia of a single super-committee of all the House's leaders in a permanent standing committee. This machinery had not existed previously in Virginia, nor in any other colony that I have found, and it undoubtedly was one factor in strengthening Virginia's cohesion in the face of the approaching storm. In a similar manner, it invited and led to creation of the first permanent, institutionalized, ongoing contact between all the colonies. Hutchinson was right; it was revolutionary, and it was not accidental.

This was the first real movement toward revolution outside of Massachusetts. Virginia had come a long way since May 1769. The speed and lack of opposition to this measure indicates two new developments. (1) Most, virtually all, of the old leaders of the House no longer placed much faith in remonstrances and petitions. Even though the Ministry had made no new assaults on colonial liberties between 1769 and the appointment of a Court of Inquiry in 1772, the arrogant and tyrannical behavior toward the City of London had not gone unnoticed. The action taken in Rhode Island looking to transport defendants for trial "beyond the seas" was the first time the King's threats had been carried into effect. No colonial leader opposing the Crown's attacks on colonial liberties could afford to ignore the threat to himself. (2) The clear evidence of collaboration between the "radicals" and Randolph indicates the breadth of their underlying agreement on the threat presented by the Crown, Ministry, and Parliament and the degree of trust they had come to have in each other.

We need not be surprised that there are no records or memoirs of such a collaboration between Randolph and the "radicals." Randolph never made any record of any of his private, behind-the-scenes politicking. Carr died two months later, in May 1773. Jefferson, Henry, and Lee were all inclined to toot their own horns and did not feel the need to hand any unnecessary credit to Randolph, who was dead within two and a half years after these events and long before their memoirs were written. We are left to draw inferences from the public acts of these men, and the inferences are those most explanatory of the known events.

There are more inferences to be drawn, perhaps the most significant. We have already seen how Randolph believed the arrogant threats made by the King, seconded promptly by Parliament, in late 1768, resulted in his bringing the "radicals" into the "government" of Virginia, bringing about a unification of the leadership against the aggressions of the British government. It is probable that the news of the appointment of a Court of Inquiry in Rhode Island caused him to conclude that a breach of some sort in the colonies' relationship with Britain was inevitable and also necessary. The resolutions of March 12, 1773, did two remarkable things.

First, the leadership of the House of Burgesses was centralized and streamlined to enable it to act with unity and to act quickly in the future. Considering the makeup of the Committee of Correspondence—the Speaker, the Treasurer, all other standing committee chairmen (the old leadership) and the leaders of the "radicals"—it is inconceivable that any measure agreed upon by this committee would not be acceptable to the House as a whole. The creation of a Select Committee residing in or very near to Williamsburg and the grant to it of authority to act for the entire committee when the House was in recess and the full Committee was unavailable, gave this new Committee of Correspondence the ability to respond with great speed when necessary, as we shall see. Randolph had observed how Virginia's ability to respond timely to the Stamp Act had been crippled by the General Assembly's having been dissolved in May 1765 as the crisis arose, allowing the Governor to prevent united action by not calling it into session until November 1766 after the crisis actually had passed. The new Committee would prevent Virginia from being similarly rendered unable to act in the future crises. Furthermore, both the full Committee and the Select Committee would be controlled by Randolph as the swing vote in the event of any disagreement. Thus, the "radicals" could not move the House farther or faster than Randolph thought prudent, but the "conservatives" could not prevent such movement forward as Randolph was willing to take. By requiring both points of view to compromise in order to gain Randolph's vote, unity was preserved. Unlike some colonies, the Virginians were all in agreement that Britain's actions were unconstitutional. The only issue between them was the nature of the cure for such actions. This fundamental agreement was a prime condition of the Virginians' unity.

Second, because Virginia took the lead in proposing committees of correspondence in all colonies and in demonstrating how their continuing communication would be useful in addressing even ordinary problems affecting more than one colony, many of the colonies that might have rejected such a suggestion coming from Massachusetts, badly tainted with a reputation for radicalism, were willing to consider and approve the suggestion with steady Virginia as its source. As the Ministry shut down one colonial legislature after another, it was the committees of correspondence that forged the links of communication and unity among the colonies.

Almost as a footnote, long after the damage to the relationship with the colonials had been done, the *Gaspee* incident faded quietly. In June 1773, the Commissioners found that witnesses' testimony had been extorted from them under duress and could not be true. They also found that the vessel's commander acting "from an intemperate, if not reprehensible zeal to aid the Custom service, exceeded the bounds of his duty." The Ministry let the investigation drop.

11

The Boston Tea Party,
December 16, 1773

By early 1773, the East India Company had 17,000,000 pounds of tea on hand, an enormous inventory.[1] Its American market had been eroded by years of controversy over the Townshend duties on tea, and merchants in New York and Philadelphia traded for tea directly with Holland in violation of the Navigation Acts. In May 1773, a Tea Act was signed, which authorized the East India Company to ship tea to its own agents or to merchants in America, at a duty of 3d (three pence, one-fourth of a shilling) per pound, payable on arrival but credited against the duty owed in Britain, which gave the East India Company an advantage over other competitors. The Ministry thereby gave concessions to the East India Company to alleviate its problem by selling directly, rather than through middle men. The Company could undercut the prices of the American merchants.[2] London newspapers said that Lord North meant to try the question of direct taxation with the Americans.[3] On July 6, 1773, Virginia's agent, Norton, wrote the Committee of Correspondence that the Ministry was making a cat's paw of the Company in order to establish the direct tax.[4] The principal merchants dealing in tea were in Boston, New York, Philadelphia, and Charleston, and the principal smugglers were in Rhode Island, New York, and Philadelphia. The Tea Act could also be used in the future to give the East India Company a monopoly on sale in America of all East Indian products. The merchants were all enraged at being cut out as the middle men. In Boston, their sense of outrage was enhanced by the appointment of Governor Hutchinson's sons as agents and consignees of the East India Company's tea.[5]

11. The Boston Tea Party, December 16, 1773

On September 27, 1773, Samuel Adams first called for a Congress of the colonies and independence.[6] This was considered another example of the extremism of the Massachusetts radicals.

The opposition to the East India Company's tea was greatest at the ports affected. In New York and Philadelphia, the Company's agents were successfully pressured to resign.[7] In Boston, the Governor and Company agents, including his sons, refused to send the tea back to Britain. The ship carrying the tea had entered the Port of Boston, and the duty became payable to Customs twenty days later, December 18. At that time, Customs could seize the tea and sell it for the duty. Hutchinson ignored all radical demands to have the ship return to England, obviously intending to force payment of the duty. As a deadline approached at which the tax would become payable whether the tea was unloaded or not, on December 16, 1773, Boston citizens superficially disguised as Indians boarded the ship at night and threw the cases of tea overboard.[8] This act of illegal violence was not approved in Virginia by Randolph, Washington, and Pendleton, nor generally.[9] It was Britain's intemperate response that drove the Virginians further toward revolution.

12

The Intolerable Acts

The British government responded promptly to the Tea Party violence. On March 25, 1774, the Commons passed the Boston Port Act. Edmund Burke spoke against it, but the Boston Tea Party had enraged almost everyone in Parliament. A motion to repeal the tax on tea was defeated 182–49. The Lords passed the bill unanimously on March 30, and the King signed the next day. It closed the Port of Boston, effective June 1, 1774, to all shipping except military vessels and cargoes of fuel and food, until Boston compensated the East India Company for the tea and gave "reasonable satisfaction" to injured revenue officers and others injured in recent riots and until the King had declared that peace and obedience had been restored so that trade might be safely conducted and duties collected. News of this Act was received in Boston on May 10, 1774.[1] Since Boston depended on shipping, mercantile trade, shipbuilding, and fishing for much of its livelihood, this Act was catastrophic for Boston. News of subsequent Acts did not reach Virginia until after the events of late May and early June, described below, so they played no part in Virginia's initial reaction.

On May 13, a convoy of additional troops arrived in Boston, and General Gage was appointed Governor to replace the native-born, though Royalist, Governor Thomas Hutchinson.[2]

On May 12, 1774, Parliament also passed the Massachusetts Government Act, which revoked the Massachusetts Charter, subjecting the colony entirely to rule by Britain. The Council was to be appointed by the King, rather than elected. The Governor could appoint and remove, without the Council's consent, all judges, justices of the peace, sheriffs, and the Attorney General. Town meetings could be held only once a year, unless with the Governor's written consent, instead of being called by the selectmen. Both grand jurors and petit jurors were to be appointed by the sheriffs, rather than by election by the Town Meeting and selection by lot from a list prepared by the selectmen, respectively. The Governor and royal officials were given immunity as to local courts. The Bill passed the Commons by 239–64 and the Lords by 57–21. Prior to this Act, colonial Acts approved by the King could not be repealed or amended by him without the colonial legislature's consent. Now Parliament claimed the right to change the laws of a colony without its consent.[3]

Parliament also passed the Massachusetts Administration of Justice Act, also known as the Coercive Act. If any soldier or official was charged with murder while suppressing a riot or collecting revenue, acting under a magistrate, he could only be tried in Britain, and witnesses could be transported to testify. This provision caused the Act to be called "the Murder Act."[4]

The Quebec Act was also passed in May 1774. It affected Virginians most directly, causing Richard Henry Lee to tell the First Continental Congress that it was the worst grievance of all. The Quebec Act annexed all land west of the Alleghenies and north of the Ohio River to the Colony of Quebec, which was governed solely by an appointed Royal Governor and Council, thus entirely subservient to the British government. It provided for support for Catholic clergy the same as under the French regime and allowed Catholics to hold Crown offices. It eliminated trial by jury in civil cases. It confirmed land tenure under French norms, by fief or seigneury, under which a vendor paid part of the sale price to the Crown and the purchaser, as a condition of approval of the sale, did homage on bended knee to the Governor as the King's representative. These provisions made Quebec unattractive to Englishmen. The New England colonies were most appalled at the enlargement and strengthening of Catholic territory adjoining them.[5]

The Quebec Act impliedly abrogated Virginia's claims, made consistently since 1612. Virginia was thus deprived of jurisdiction north of the Ohio River. Since the territory was in the Empire, Parliament would be able to make a grant to the Grand Ohio (Walpole) Company. All Virginia's claims in this territory were revoked, possibly even including those of the veterans of 1754. As for land west of the mountains and south of the Ohio River, it was all considered Crown lands except for that which had been lawfully granted since January 1774. It was under direct military rule, as had been the case since the Proclamation of 1763.

On June 2, 1774, the Quartering Act was amended. In 1769, the Massachusetts House had refused to vote supplies for troops quartered in the colony. The amendment provided that, if a colony had not provided barracks for troops, they could be quartered in uninhabited or other buildings, which allowed the quartering of troops in private residences. "Reasonable" compensation was to be paid. A householder could be required to house one or more soldiers in the midst of his family with consequent risk to himself, his wife, and daughters of insolent or violent behavior on the part of his "guests" which could also endanger his property. The manner in which Louis XIV had quartered troops in the residences of Protestants was still remembered. Lord Chatham (Pitt) spoke against the bill, but it passed the Lords 57–16.[6]

Still later in June, the Quebec Revenue Act was passed. It discriminated against the colonies in favor of Quebec, Britain, Ireland, and the British West Indies. Duty on rum (used in the Indian trade) was made higher on rum distilled in the colonies than on rum distilled in the British West Indies. Duty on molasses imported in ships owned in the colonies was made higher than duty shipped in bottoms owned in Quebec, Britain, or Ireland. Articles subject to duty imported to Quebec could be cleared by Customs in Quebec City or else had to be cleared at St. John's, Quebec (now in Prince Edward Island). A Philadelphia merchant importing rum for sale to Indians in the Ohio Valley (now in Quebec), thus had to clear Customs in St. John's, while his competitor in Quebec City cleared Customs a few blocks from his warehouse. Some of the supporters of the Quebec Act stated an intent to please the French Canadians, against the eventuality that they could be enlisted to put down rebellion in the other colonies.[7]

13

The May 5, 1774,
General Assembly

A Day of Fasting and Prayer,
Dissolution and Response

The General Assembly convened on May 5, 1774. Between May 16 and 18, a ship from Britain brought news of the closing of the Port of Boston, effective June 1. The Burgesses were furious. Landon Carter said that Parliament had declared war on Boston. "This is a prelude to destroy the liberties of America."[1] A letter from Arthur Lee in London was handed around, reporting that Lord North had told the Lords that "he would not listen to the complaint of America till she was at his feet."[2] No news had arrived directly from Boston, but it was eagerly awaited. Randolph controlled the calendar of the House and kept the House at work on its regular business. To prevent a dissolution, debate on the events in Boston would have to wait, which would also give the House time to receive more accurate news, in the face of a multitude of exciting rumors. News of the subsequent Intolerable Acts had not arrived. Everyone realized that the House's support of Boston would bring on a dissolution by the Governor.

One routine piece of business was the necessity for renewing the appropriation for the courts, the prior appropriation having expired in April. In order to prevent creditors, particularly British creditors, from collecting their debts, Richard Henry Lee successfully defeated the effort by Pendleton and some other conservatives to pass a new Act for the courts. This effectively closed all the courts in Virginia.[3] The intent was to pressure British merchants.

102

The radicals caucused, searching for some action that would arouse the colony without bringing on a dissolution. No one wanted to cause a dissolution until news of Boston's response had arrived, so the Burgesses could fashion Virginia's response with Boston's before them.

Richard Henry Lee, Henry, Frank Lee, Jefferson, Mason, and two or three others arrived at the idea of proclaiming June 1, the day the Port of Boston was to be closed, as a Day of Fasting and Prayer throughout the colony. They did not believe that Governor Dunmore would respond harshly to a call for prayer. The evening of May 23 they met in the Council Chamber in the Capitol in order to search the records, especially the acts of Parliament against Charles I. A resolution was drawn in the rhetoric of the seventeenth century. June 1 was to be a Day of Fasting and Prayer

Governor John Murray, 4th Earl of Dunmore, **Sir Joshua Reynolds, 18th century oil on canvas (National Galleries of Scotland, Edinburgh, United Kingdom, No. PG2895. Purchased 1992 with contributions from the Art Fund and the National Heritage Memorial Fund).**

to avert "destruction of our civil rights and the evils of civil war; to give us one heart and one mind firmly to oppose, by all just and proper means, every injury to American rights." In order to emphasize the purported religious nature of the resolution, the radicals called on Treasurer Robert Carter Nicholas, widely known for his piety, to introduce the resolution. He agreed, and on May 24 he did so. It passed without a dissenting voice.[4]

The fact that Nicholas, a staunch "conservative," would present the "radicals'" resolution speaks volumes as to the "temperature" of the House. In their haste to "do something," the radicals' selected method of protest required that they not wait longer. If June 1 were to be the Day of Fasting and Prayer, they had to move forward with their resolution promptly. Even five days of riding was not enough to give notice to all the counties in Virginia and allow them to prepare an appropriate ceremony, so they had to move no later than May 24.

Thomas Jefferson, **Mather Brown, oil on canvas, 1786 (National Portrait Gallery, Smithsonian Institution, No. NPG.99.66 Jefferson R.tif. Bequest of Charles Francis Adams).**

Dissolution and the Call for Convention

Governor Dunmore dissolved the Burgesses on May 26. Landon Carter was outraged that a resolution to pray was sufficient cause for the Governor, but certainly the language of the resolution should have raised the possibility in the minds of the radicals. Nevertheless, personal enmity toward the Governor was not in the Virginians' minds or habits. Washington had dinner with Dunmore the evening of May 25 and rode out to Dunmore's farm with him for breakfast the next morning, the day Dunmore dissolved the House. The day after the dissolution, a previously scheduled ball in the Governor's honor was held, at which all the Virginia ladies wore Virginia-spun cloth.[5]

With the meeting at the Raleigh Tavern following the Burgesses' dissolution in 1769 as a precedent, on May 27, the day after dissolution, eighty-nine Burgesses met at Raleigh Tavern, where they again elected Randolph as Moderator. They organized themselves into a new Association and denounced the Boston Port Act. Lee proposed an agreement not to import tea, but the new Association agreed to boycott all products of the East India Company except spice and saltpeter (for gunpowder). They resolved, "an attack made on one of our sister Colonies ... is an attack made on all British America.... [I]t is recommended to the Committee on Correspondence that they communicate with their several corresponding Committees, on the Expediency of appointing Deputies from the several Colonies of British America to meet in general Congress at such place annually as shall be thought most convenient." They also warned that unconstitutional taxation may compel Virginia to avoid all trade with Britain.[6] Acting without news from Boston, the Associators proceeded moderately.

On May 28, Randolph called a meeting of the full Committee of Correspondence to prepare a letter to the other colonies, consulting them on the desirability of holding annual Congresses. They instructed the Select Committee to have the letters in the post that same day.[7]

May 29 was a Sunday. Late in the day, a messenger arrived with a parcel for Randolph. It contained letters from the Philadelphia and Annapolis Committees of Correspondence, containing copies of the proceedings of a Boston Town Meeting held on May 13, signed by Samuel Adams. Boston wrote that they could not stand alone and asked for a general agreement among the North American colonies to stop imports and exports of all goods from Britain and the British West Indies until the Port of Boston was reopened. Boston did not request a Congress. Philadelphia would not agree to a non-importation and non-exportation agreement unless a Congress met and tried reconciliation first. The Committee in Annapolis also suggested closing all colonial courts to British creditors.[8] The delivery of Boston's appeal was slowed to sixteen days by the time required for the Committees of two other colonies to meet, act, and forward Boston's appeal with their own action thereon attached. Virginia had already acted more vigorously even than Boston had requested. The Associators had already agreed to boycott the East India Company, while the others sought an agreement by all the colonies before stopping any trade. Before knowing that any other colony had requested a Congress, the Virginians had already proposed not just a Congress but an annual Congress.

13. The May 5, 1774, General Assembly

Randolph summoned all members of the full Committee of Correspondence and also all other Burgesses still in town or in the area, to meet the next day, May 30, at the Raleigh Tavern. Twenty-four or twenty-five Burgesses, acting as "Associators," assembled, including Washington, Jefferson, Pendleton, Nicholas, Mason, and Thomas Nelson, Jr. Randolph served as Moderator of the meeting. Those present agreed that the non-importation terms should be broadened, but they disagreed on whether exports should be embargoed. Henry, Lee, Mason, and, now, Nicholas favored a complete embargo on imports and exports, moratorium on debt payments to Britain, and the closing of colonial courts. Randolph and Pendleton favored a non-importation agreement and would consider an embargo on exports after a year if Britain had not backed down but not on this year's exports, since the new tobacco crop was already in the ground. They agreed that they had no authority to enlarge the terms adopted by the full Association three days earlier. Since they had no authority to convene the Burgesses, they unanimously called for a "Convention" of the new Association, consisting of almost all former Burgesses, to meet in Williamsburg on August 1, 1774, to review Virginia's response to the Boston Port Act. On May 31, the call for Convention, signed by Randolph, Nicholas, and Pendleton, was printed together with Boston's call for help. Randolph wrote, "Things seem to be hurrying to an alarming crisis and demand the speedy united council of all those who have regard for the common cause."[9]

Randolph convened the Select Committee of the Committee of Correspondence. The reports from Boston, Philadelphia, and Annapolis with Virginia's response were sent south to North Carolina and thence to South Carolina and Georgia. The Select Committee reported Virginia's actions back to Annapolis, and thence to Philadelphia and on north through the other colonies to Boston.[10]

At the end of this extraordinary week, on June 1, 1774, Randolph

and the Clerk bearing the Mace led the available Burgesses and citizens of Williamsburg to a service of Prayer at Bruton Parish Church, the Court Church of the capital. Fasting and services of prayer were held all over Virginia.[11]

While New York refused to participate in a non-importation agreement, they had suggested a Congress. Connecticut and Rhode Island joined in doing so during early June. With the unequivocal support of Virginia and its New England neighbors, on June 17, the Massachusetts House instructed its Speaker to invite all colonies to send delegates to Philadelphia on September 1.

Some writers go out of their way to try to make Randolph look timid, or too conservative, or worse. A closer examination of what happened does not justify that criticism. From the time the news of closing the Port of Boston arrived, Randolph kept a close rein on the calendar of issues brought to the floor, in order to avoid a dissolution before the Burgesses learned what had been done in Boston. Virginia should not act before knowing how Boston had responded. If the radicals had not pushed the Fasting and Prayer measure, the Burgesses would have been in session when Randolph received his parcel five days later. As in 1769, Randolph could have then taken the Burgesses into secret session to forestall a premature dissolution, and Virginia's response could have been dealt with legally through the Burgesses. While the authority of the Burgesses was limited, due to the necessity of getting the agreement of the Council and the Governor's signature for an action by the entire General Assembly, a delay to learn of Boston's response would have been valuable. If Dunmore dissolved the Assembly after the House had voted in secret session on a response Dunmore did not like, the 1769 precedent was for a new Association. Had it acted after Boston's response was known, a much broader non-importation agreement would have been put into effect two months earlier than a Convention was able to meet. Dunmore was obviously aware of the prior tactics used in 1769 and dissolved the House when its intent became clear and they gave him an excuse. This is a case in which the radicals had their way, but the result was self-defeating. Nevertheless, with feelings running so high, Randolph allowed the Fasting and Prayer measure to come to the floor; it received approval without a dissent, and it would have been too great a cost, politically, for Randolph to try to stick his thumb in the dyke. In other words, he did not try to hold back the radicals when they had such a large majority at their backs. While their "victory" had some value in stirring up the colony, a price was paid in delaying Virginia's full response, which, had it been known in other colonies, might have affected their responses.

The 1769 organization of an Association set the precedent for the same action in 1774. The Associators went further on their non-importation agreement than Lee had requested, enlarging the non-importation to cover all East India Company products instead of just tea. The importance of the legal structure set up by the enlarged Committee of Correspondence is underlined by the Associators' "recommendation" to the Committee that it communicate with the other colonies' Committees regarding annual Congresses. Randolph's procedural skill is again noticeable in the suggestion of annual Congresses, eliminating the cumbersomeness and possible failure to organize a new Congress for each emergency. With annual Congresses, the creation of an institutional structure for revolution was greatly advanced. The Association did not purport to control the legal machinery of the Burgesses; at this stage, they were two separate entities with essentially identical memberships.

The rapidity with which Randolph acted after receiving Boston's plea for help is truly remarkable. It could not be improved upon. The available Burgesses were summoned by Randolph as Moderator of the Association. The meeting had the nature of a joint meeting of the Committee of Correspondence and the Association. The Associators decided they did not have authority to change the terms of the non-importation agreement adopted in the full meeting of Associators only three days earlier. Despite the dual nature of the meeting on May 30, the legitimacy of its actions was not in question. It was as the Committee of Correspondence that a response was determined, and the drafting of the response was turned over to the Select Committee of the Committee of Correspondence. It was Randolph who preserved the legitimacy of the actions taken, lest there be a revolutionary action or action by a mob, no matter how distinguished its members.

Randolph was Moderator of the Association, Speaker and Chairman of the standing Committee of Correspondence. It was as Moderator that he called the Association's members into session on May 30. The Association issued the call for Convention, and the Convention was to be a Convention of the Association. The delegates were all members of the dissolved Burgesses, at the time the call was made, but the counties could hold meetings of the local members who agreed to sign the Association and "instruct" their delegate to the Convention. At this point in time, and later at this first Virginia Convention, the Convention did not seek to act as a legislative body. Nevertheless, this was a significant extra-constitutional action by the Association that May 30. There can be no question that Randolph guided the decision to issue the call for a Convention. This was a matter squarely within his own cognizance, whether as Moderator, Speaker, or Chairman of the Committee of Correspondence. The radicals had had their day, made possible by the extreme heat generated by notice of the Boston Port Act, and now it was Randolph's decisions that guided the meetings of May 27 through May 30. The radicals would not have a free hand again. In view of the consequences this time, it was well that they did not.

14

The August 1, 1774, Convention

Between the time of the call for an August 1 Convention and the day it convened, numerous county meetings were held to give instructions to their members. The great turnout for these meetings was unprecedented. The resolutions passed in these meetings were uniformly very hostile toward Britain. They insisted on Virginia's sole right to tax itself and denounced the Ministry's attacks on liberty. They generally favored non-importation, and a few favored a ban on exports. They also expressed a willingness to take united action with the other colonies. During the summer, news of the "Murder Act," the Massachusetts Government Act, the Coercive Act, the Quebec Act, and the Quartering Act further inflamed the Virginians.[1] In June 1774, Committees of Safety began to be formed to enforce the new non-importation agreement.[2] Before the Convention met, John Randolph published a pamphlet urging restraint and petition.

Governor Dunmore sought to derail the Convention by calling for election of Burgesses and a General Assembly to convene on August 11. Randolph prevented delay and confusion by announcing, as Moderator, that any new Burgesses elected for the August 11 General Assembly would be seated in the Convention on August 1.[3] Dunmore then called up the militia of the frontier counties for an Indian campaign, leaving in mid–July, and many of the Burgesses from the Western counties were absent on his campaign. As he left Williamsburg in mid–July, he postponed the new General Assembly to November. (He later postponed it to June 1, 1775.) Having done what he could to disrupt the Convention, he then left the capital.[4]

Nevertheless, more than 100 delegates met in Convention on August 1. Randolph was again elected Moderator. Every delegate was a member of the old House or had been elected to the new House. Randolph appointed two committees, one to draft amendments to the May 27, 1774, Articles of Association and one to draft instructions to delegates to a continental Congress. Jefferson, who was sick, had sent Randolph "A Summary View of the Rights of British America." Randolph had this laid on the table, and then directed that it be printed, thereby distancing himself from his brother John Randolph's views.[5]

After a week of deliberation, on August 6, the Convention adopted new Articles of Association. All imports, except medicine, were to be halted as of November 1, 1774, and all exports were to be halted on August 10, 1775. (The 1774 tobacco crop had been planted, and it could not be marketed until the summer of 1775.) Slaves were included on the non-importation list. No tea still on hand would be used after November 1, 1774. Merchants who refused to sign were to be boycotted by all signers and "well-wishers" of the Colony. Those who exported after August 10, 1775, would be considered "inimical to the community and as an approver of American grievances."[6] The Courts remained closed in order to pressure the British merchants and to protect Virginia planters who were being squeezed by non-importation and the threat of non-exportation. The Convention encouraged County Committees to send relief to the poor of Boston. Sheep weaned before May 1 could not be exported, to encourage weaving.

After Committees of Correspondence for New York, Philadelphia, Providence, Virginia, and Connecticut had called for a Congress, the Massachusetts House had its Speaker invite all to a Congress in Philadelphia on September 1.[7] On August 5, the Convention agreed to send delegates to the Congress.[8] Very significantly, the Convention authorized creation of independent county militias, not under the control of a Royal Governor.[9]

The instructions for delegates to the Congress declared Parliament's acts unconstitutional. "Of this nature we consider the several acts of Parliament for raising revenue in America, for extending the jurisdiction of the courts of Admiralty, for seizing American subjects and transporting them to Britain to be tried for offenses in America and the several late oppressive acts respecting the town of Boston and the province of the Massachusetts Bay." General Gage was criticized for denying the right of assembly in Massachusetts and for claiming powers for himself not claimed even by the King.[10] The delegates should support united action to stop all imports on November 1, 1774, and all exports as of August 10, 1775. The Convention agreed to conform to other actions of Congress to which Virginia's delegates agreed.[11] Randolph was elected chairman of the Virginia delegation. The other delegates were Washington and Henry, tied for second place, Lee, Pendleton, Harrison, and Bland, in that order. There were three "radicals," three "conservatives," and Randolph. The radicals all placed ahead of the conservatives. (Some claimed that Washington had offered to raise 1,000 men at his own expense and lead them to Boston.[12])

Randolph was empowered as Moderator to reconvene the Convention at such time and place as, in his opinion, circumstances required. In event of his death, Robert Carter Nicholas could do so.

Before the Convention adjourned, a number of delegates, undoubtedly including the seven elected as delegates to the Congress, met at Randolph's house. Jefferson's *Summary* was read out loud to the group, to general though not universal applause to the entirety of its argument. Most notable were Jefferson's condemnation of the King's power to suspend colonial legislation until his approval was given and the restriction of Virginia's right to trade with other nations and Jefferson's denial that Parliament had any rights in Virginia at all. Jefferson's *Summary* was intended as instructions to

Benjamin Harrison V, (1726–1791), unidentified artist, watercolor on ivory, 18th century miniature painted from life (Virginia Historical Society, No. 1968.28.1A-B).

113

the delegates to Congress.[13] Though Randolph had called it to the attention of the Convention, it was never brought before it for that purpose, since it would have injected lengthy controversy. By having it read in its entirety, twenty-three pages, at his own house, Randolph clearly endorsed it publicly. It was by far the most radical and revolutionary presentation of the arguments against Britain's oppressive behavior and the most extreme assertion of Virginia's rights. All the delegates to Congress were thereby exposed to the enthusiastic response to the reading of this extraordinary document.

Many radicals had desired a cessation of exports after sale of the current crop, a position supported by very few county conventions. Randolph and others regarded such a measure as punitive primarily to Virginia and successfully delayed for a year the embargo on exports. The Congress would adopt their position. The radicals, again, pressed to go too fast for the Colony. Who would doubt that Randolph had a

Above: Peyton Randolph House, exterior, Williamsburg (Colonial Williamsburg Foundation, No. 1999-1336). *Opposite top: Peyton Randolph House, Dining Room, Williamsburg* (Colonial Williamsburg Foundation, No. T2000-924). *Opposite bottom: Peyton Randolph House, Library, Williamsburg* (Colonial Williamsburg Foundation, No. DS1999-317).

hand in this decision? Indeed, some writers complain that he was too cautious. Cautious in presiding over a Convention which began the creation of armed forces independent of the King and Governor? And in sponsoring the reading in his own home of Jefferson's revolutionary tract? It seems probable that, by this point, if not sooner, Randolph had concluded that force was the most likely outcome of all these events.

Lord Dunmore's War

During the ten years following the end of the French and Indian War, despite the failure to obtain clear title, thousands of settlers streamed into the area around Fort Pitt. Braddock's Road gave access to the Monongahela and the Ohio Valley for settlers from Virginia and Maryland. Forbes' Road from Carlisle to Fort Pitt gave access to settlers from Pennsylvania and New Jersey. A large number of the 1754 veterans' grants had been surveyed, and some "settled," along the Monongahela River, the southerly of the two rivers that join at Pittsburgh to become the Ohio River. Other veterans' grants and many "headright" grants were located on the south side of the Ohio and its tributaries in the present States of West Virginia and Pennsylvania. These settlers had titles; the squatters were relying on past experience of squatters being given the opportunity to perfect their claims.

Since the Proclamation of 1763, Britain's military rule of all land west of the Alleghenies had been enforced in the Fort Pitt area by the garrison and its commander, who permitted the Philadelphia interest to trade with the Indians of the Ohio Valley. In 1772, the British evacuated and dismantled Fort Pitt, in order to concentrate their forces dealing with colonial unrest. (So much for Britain's claim that a permanent military establishment was necessary to protect the colonists from the Indians!) By 1773, Pennsylvania was asserting its own later, conflicting claim to the area. In February 1773, Pennsylvania created Westmoreland County, which included the area around Fort Pitt. When the settlers petitioned Pennsylvania to reestablish the fort or even organize a militia for protection against Indians, their petition was ignored.

In August 1773, Governor Dunmore traveled to Fort Pitt to assess conditions on the frontier, especially since patents for titles were finally beginning to be issued for the Western lands. He estimated that more than 10,000 settlers were in the area claimed by Virginia, living without any magistrates or organized militia and, now that Fort Pitt had been abandoned, with no organized protection from the Indians.[14] Lord Dunmore organized a new West District of Augusta County, covering much of the same territory as Westmoreland County. He appointed John Connolly and six other local men as magistrates, created a county militia and appointed Connolly as Captain. Four hundred settlers signed a petition condemning Pennsylvania and requesting Virginia's support.[15] Connolly appeared in Fort Pitt on January 1, 1774, exhibited his commission and proclaimed the new West District of Augusta County. The Pennsylvania magistrate arrested him. He was freed on bond, returned to Staunton (the county seat of Augusta County), and received a commission as Justice of Augusta County. He reappeared at Fort Pitt on March 5, 1774. Pursuant to Lord Dunmore's order, the newly organized militia seized the site of Fort Pitt, renaming it Fort Dunmore.[16] Connolly sent a militia unit to Hannastown, where they broke up a session of the Westmoreland (Pennsylvania) County Court. That spring, arrests were followed by counter-arrests.[17]

Indian fighting began in the area in early 1774. When the General Assembly met on May 5, Governor Dunmore sent a message to the Burgesses. "[H]e informs them that a considerable body of His Majesty's subjects had settled in Virginia, contiguous to the western boundary of Pennsylvania; that he had appointed militia officers to defend them on any emergency and magistrates to preserve order; that the governor of Pennsylvania pretended a claim to that country; that he [Dunmore] had taken steps to enforce the authority of Virginia in that district; and that he submits to the House, as the governor of Pennsylvania meant to obstruct by every possible means the government of this colony in the disputed district, if provisions be not necessary to render the legal power of the officers and magistrates there effectual."[18] The next day, he sent the House several letters from Connolly, describing Indian outrages. The Burgesses rejected Dunmore's request for regular Virginia troops, but they enthusiastically authorized a militia expedition to pacify the Indians and safeguard the new frontier settlers. We may credit Dunmore with a desire to protect his colony's claims in the West, along with his personal investment in those lands. We may also credit him with using a popular expedition to interfere with the August 1, 1774, Convention, as we have seen. He undoubtedly hoped that Virginians' approval of his expedition would divert them from supporting the Massachusetts radicals.

We may further credit Lord Dunmore, an able representative of the Crown, with seeking to sow dissension between two of the three largest colonies, Virginia and Pennsylvania, on the eve and during the commencement of the Continental Congress. I doubt that his organization of a new County district in August 1773 was done with this in mind, since the calls for a Congress did not commence until May 1774. However, by the time he issued a call in early June for 2,600 militia of the frontier counties to prepare for the campaign, only days after the meetings of May 27–30, that purpose would have been added.[19] He did not fool all Virginians about his intentions. On May 20, 1774, Landon Carter wrote, "Lord Dunmore wants 1,200 men to fight the Pennsylvanians. I'd rather raise them for Boston a great deal."[20] By the time he left Williamsburg in mid–July, other colonies had joined Virginia in calling for a Congress, and the convening of one was almost a certainty.

Governor Dunmore's expedition against the Indians was successful, decisively turning back the Shawnee at Point Pleasant. The Shawnee gave up their claims south of the Ohio, opening the entry into central Kentucky. The point of departure for his Ohio campaign was Fort Pitt in September 1774, and the battle at Point Pleasant was on October 10, overlapping the period during which the Continental Congress convened in Philadelphia, commencing September 5. His militia also captured Hannastown, the seat of Westmoreland County, and arrested three Pennsylvania magistrates who refused to take an oath of allegiance to Virginia.[21] He successfully established Fort Pitt as a Virginia frontier post. Five years later, George Rogers Clark, leading a force of Virginia militia, launched his Western campaign that drove the British out of the Ohio Valley from a Virginia base at Fort Pitt.

Thus, Governor Dunmore succeeded in converting a territorial dispute between Virginia and Pennsylvania into a dispute resolved by legal compulsion and, finally, by military force. The clear intent was to estrange the two colonies, if not create a war between them, in order to interfere with the Continental Congress or, at least, to foreclose cooperation between the two colonies. Dunmore was obviously aware that powerful men in Pennsylvania were personally interested in land speculation in Western Pennsylvania and the Ohio Valley and would view this action by Virginia as being hostile to them personally.

15

The First Continental Congress, September 5, 1774

The First Continental Congress convened on September 5, 1774, in Philadelphia. Every colony sent delegates except Georgia; a total of fifty-five delegates were present. Randolph, Lee, Bland, and Harrison were the first Virginia delegates to arrive on September 1. On their way to Philadelphia, Bland made it clear that he was determined not to yield. They had important work to do before the Congress opened. Washington, Henry, and Pendleton arrived on September 4, the day before the Congress convened. Henry and Pendleton traveled together to join Washington for the journey to Philadelphia. George Mason joined them to confer the night they spent at Mt. Vernon. As the three delegates prepared to leave the next morning, Martha Washington told Pendleton, "God be with you gentlemen. I hope you will stand firm. I know George will."[1]

The colony of Pennsylvania was divided. The "reconcilers" objected to the call for a Congress, and the Pennsylvania legislature was in their hands. Their Speaker was Joseph Galloway, the spokesman for the Whartons and the Grand Ohio Company. The Pennsylvania delegation included John Dickinson, also active in the Grand Ohio Company. The reconcilers included Dickinson, Charles Humphreys, John Morton, and Samuel Rhoades. Galloway and his allies controlled the delegation. The radical minority in the delegation were Thomas Mifflin, John Bubenheim Bayard, and Edward Biddle. The Pennsylvania Assembly had instructed the delegates to adopt a plan to obtain a redress of grievances but to avoid disrespect to Britain. As other colonies' delegates arrived, the majority offered the State House, controlled by themselves, as the best accommodation in which the Congress could meet. The "radicals" offered the recently completed Carpenters' Hall, which they controlled. One of their leaders, not in the delegation, was Charles Thomson.[2]

The New York delegation bore unimpressive credentials. The New

Carpenters' Hall, exterior, Philadelphia (courtesy Carpenters' Company, Philadelphia).

Carpenters' Hall, interior, Philadelphia (**courtesy Carpenters' Company, Philadelphia**).

York Assembly had made no effort to convene to elect delegates. The delegates had been selected by an ad hoc Committee of Correspondence; only one member of the New York delegation was a member of its Assembly.[3]

Lee, who had previously corresponded with the leader of the Massachusetts delegation, Samuel Adams, conducted the discussions and negotiations with Samuel Adams, his cousin, John Adams, Thomas Lynch of South Carolina, and, presumably, a representative of the Pennsylvania radicals. These conversations took place over the days before the Congress met. Lee met with the entire Massachusetts delegation on September 3. While Lee was the front man, there can be no doubt that the other three Virginia delegates then present participated with Lee in determining on a strategy. Randolph was clearly the most experienced legislator in the Congress, and the two Adamses regarded him, by reputation and by their short acquaintance with him, as also the best legal mind present.[4]

The delegates in a group viewed the Carpenter's Hall accommodations on September 5. As they did so, Thomas Lynch of South Carolina proposed that they sit in it, which was approved by acclamation. The Congress would meet on friendly ground. When the delegates were seated, Lynch nominated Randolph as chairman and was seconded by Samuel Adams. Randolph was elected unanimously. He took the chair and nodded to Lynch, who then proposed that Charles Thomson be appointed as Secretary. Thomson entered the hall, on cue, and was appointed. This gave the Pennsylvania radicals a prominent seat in the Congress. The delegates settled on "President" as the official title of their chairman. Randolph then called on the delegates to present their credentials and had the Secretary read the delegates' credentials into the record.[5] There can be no doubt that Randolph had a hand in the planning. Radical, unpopular Massachusetts appeared to be a minor mover in these decisions. As John Adams wrote at the time, "We have a delicate course to steer between too much activity and too much insensibility in our critical, interested situation. We have been obliged to act with great delicacy and caution ... to keep ourselves out of sight ... to insinuate our sentiments, designs and desires by means of other persons, sometimes of one province and sometimes of another."[6]

After a heated debate, the first of the Congress, it was decided to have votes counted by colony, the majority of that colony's delegates determining how its vote would go. Patrick Henry had vehemently asserted the right of the large colonies to have a proportionate vote in the Congress, but he was not in touch with the mood of the delegates and was overruled. Harrison supported him, but Bland spoke against him. Washington remained silent during the debate. The next day, the Congress established two committees: (1) a committee to define the colonies' rights and determine how infringed rights could be restored, with two delegates from each colony and (2) a committee to report on acts of Parliament affecting the colonies' trade and manufactures, with one delegate from each colony.[7] Henry's unpredictability lost him a seat on the principal committee, to which Lee and Pendleton were elected by the Virginia delegation, but he was awarded a seat on the lesser committee.

Early in September, as the Congress was just getting organized, they learned from dispatches brought by Paul Revere, that on September 1, General Gage had seized Massachusetts' powder stored at Charlestown, across the river from Boston, and had fortified the neck of the peninsula on which Boston was built. As the committees were at work, on September 17, the Congress received a copy of the "Suffolk Resolves," adopted by the meeting of Suffolk County (Boston), Massachusetts, which provided: (1) If leaders of the popular cause were arrested, all royal officers should be seized and held until their release. (2) A Massachusetts congress should withhold taxes, cease obedience to royal judges and sheriffs, form a militia, and stop trade with Britain, Ireland, and the British West Indies. (3) Massachusetts would never submit to repression but would "have no inclination to commence a war with His Majesty's troops." The Congress unanimously approved Massachusetts' conduct and perseverance and hoped that united effort would effect a change in Britain.[8] Note that the Congress approved Boston's conduct, not its proposals, and that the stated course of action would be united action to effect a change in Britain's attitude. That could mean anything from united action in petition and remonstrance to any other imaginable course of action. The Congress had unanimously voted to say nothing of consequence, disclosing the delegates' state of mind at this early point in the Congress. The leaders of the party seeking some way clear to reconciliation were Pennsylvania and New York, and the Congress were closely divided.

On the next day, September 18, the Congress endorsed military training. Lee had proposed further that each county's militia be well supplied with arms and ammunition. He failed to carry even the Virginia delegation with him; Harrison objected that it would irritate to carry the matter this additional step.[9] Lee, once again, was ahead of most Virginians as well as the Congress. Both Virginia and the Congress were opposed to Britain's actions, but neither was prepared to consider war, and both hoped to avoid it.

On September 26, Lee moved a resolution for non-importation of any goods from Britain and Ireland, nor should any such goods be used or bought. Merchants were to give no new orders and to suspend orders already given and not yet received. The Virginia Convention had proposed November 1, 1774, as the effective date. Henry spoke for

December 1 as the effective date, which passed. No delegate spoke against non-importation. The King's signature of the Quebec Act on June 22 had caused most Whig delegates to recognize that something more than petitions would be required. The resolution passed unanimously on September 27. As significant as the decision to adopt some form of non-importation rule was the decision that it would apply, not just to those who agreed to it, but also to all others who would be required not to use or buy such imported goods after the effective date.[10]

Galloway, John Jay and James Duane of New York, and Edward Rutledge of South Carolina sought to render ineffective the Congress whose creation they had opposed, except as a tool of reconciliation. The very next day, on September 28, they brought forward a superficially attractive proposal to create a union of the colonies, to be governed by a Grand Council. The Grand Council would meet at least annually, presided over by a President General appointed and removable by the King. It would have jurisdiction over some matters now subject to the colonial legislatures, but all legislative authority would rest in the Grand Council and Parliament jointly. Finally, and critically, the present Congress would defer action to secure redress of their grievances until the King and Parliament acted on this proposal. None of the colonial legislatures had considered or authorized any such union. The proposal appeared to be "nationalistic" and demonstrated an apparent spirit of mutual affection and support among the colonies. Some of the delegates were attracted to it, and it had the support of those who sought reconciliation with Britain above all else and would have limited the Congress to petition and remonstrance. The intent of the authors, and its potential effect, was to undermine the significance of the Congress, and to prevent it taking any action at its current session. The razor's edge on which the Virginians and their allies worked was demonstrated by the vote on September 28 of 6–5 to table the proposal. The votes were not then there to defeat it outright.[11] As John Adams wrote, "Delegates are fixed against hostilities and rupture, except they should become absolutely necessary; and this necessity they do not yet see."

Having tabled Galloway's proposal, on September 30 the Congress approved non-exportation to Britain, Ireland, and the British West Indies, effective September 10, 1775. It then approved a Committee to bring in a detailed plan. Cushing, Low, and Mifflin, merchants of Boston, New York, and Philadelphia respectively, Lee, and Henry Johnson, a Maryland lawyer, were appointed.[12]

On October 3, Lee returned to the subject of the militia. He proposed that the Congress recommend to the several colonies that they appoint militias with arms and ammunition. He was supported by Henry, Roger Sherman, and Eliphalet Dyer of Connecticut and Thomas Lynch of South Carolina. Harrison again opposed the motion, saying that "Our business is to reconcile." Pendleton and Bland supported Harrison, as well as both Edward and John Rutledge of South Carolina, Duane and Low of New York, and William Hooper of North Carolina. The resolution adopted on October 3 said: "The colonial militia, if put upon a proper footing, would be sufficient to their defense in time of peace; that they are desirous of putting it on such footing immediately, and that in case of war the colonies are ready to grant supplies for raising any other forces that may be necessary."[13] Within the Virginia delegation, Randolph's vote was necessary to break the tie in the delegation in favor of Lee's motion. Within the Congress as a whole, the passage of a militia measure stronger than the one rejected on September 26 indicates a firming of sentiment against Britain. Who counted the votes and found they had shifted since September 26?

The Massachusetts Committee of Correspondence had asked the Congress how they should deal with the military rule of Massachusetts. A Congressional committee drafted a protest to General Gage. Then, on October 6, Congress formally advised Massachusetts that it approved their resistance. If actions were imposed by force, all America should join in opposition. The people were encouraged not to leave Boston, but if Massachusetts decided it was necessary for them to do so, all Americans should help support them. If the courts could not operate under Massachusetts' charter and law, they should be closed. All persons who served the military government should be shunned.[14] The October 6 vote confirmed the firmer mood of the Congress.

The Committee brought in its detailed plan for enforcing non-importation. The plan was for an Association of "Committees of

Inspection," to be elected in every county, city, and town by those qualified to vote for the colonial legislature. The local committees would publish the names of those violating the non-importation rules of the Association, who would then be ostracized by Association members. A central Committee of Correspondence in each colony was to inspect Custom house entries and report to other Committees of Correspondence. Any colony not participating would be cut off from trade by the other colonies. Effective immediately, no sheep were to be exported. Effective December 2, 1774, no goods of any kind were to be imported from Britain and Ireland, nor East India tea from anywhere. No slaves could be imported effective December 2. Beginning March 1, 1775, no goods of the types prohibited could be used or purchased. Effective September 10, 1775, no goods were to be exported to Britain, Ireland, or the West Indies, except rice to Europe. On October 12 the Committee's plan was adopted.[15] A smooth copy was prepared and signed by the members of the Congress on October 20.

On October 14, preliminary approval was given to a Declaration of Rights and Grievances.[16] The Congress petitioned the King and the people of Britain, but not Parliament, for relief of their grievances.[17] Congress had heard the affidavit of a Bostonian who had been seized in Boston and transported to London, charged with encouraging British sailors to desert, was there interrogated and finally released for insufficient evidence. On October 21, a resolution was passed that all attempts to seize colonials for transportation should be resisted and subjected to reprisal.[18]

On October 22, the votes were now available, and Galloway's Grand Council proposal was rejected.[19] Having disposed of Galloway's Grand Council plan, the Congress then asked the colonies to select delegates to a Second Continental Congress to meet in Philadelphia on May 10, 1775.[20]

The Congress's work was nearly done when, on October 23, most of the Virginia delegation, including Randolph, left for Williamsburg to attend the new General Assembly called by Governor Dunmore. Henry gave Lee his proxy, and the other delegates gave theirs to Washington.[21] Henry Middleton of South Carolina was elected President to succeed Randolph for the few days remaining. The Congress adjourned on October 26.

The main achievement of the Congress was its adoption of Articles of Association and election of local Committees (of Association or of Safety or of Inspection) to enforce the embargo in every county and town in the colonies. In effect, the Congress approved the creation of new, parallel structures of government throughout the colonies, structures no longer subject to royal control or veto. The Associations were modeled on Virginia's non-importation agreement and the means of enforcement created during May–August 1774. All exports to Britain, Ireland, and the British West Indies were to cease, effective September 10, 1775. Any colony not joining the Association would be boycotted. A major condition of Virginia's support, equally desired by Maryland and North Carolina, was met by the postponement of a prohibition on exports. Similar concessions were made for South Carolina's exports of indigo and the allowance, without time limit, of its export of rice to other European countries and their colonies.[22] The effectiveness of the Congress's work was recognized by Governor Dunmore's statement in December 1774: "There is not a Justice of the Peace in Virginia that acts, except as a Committee-man."[23] Its work was rejected in Britain, setting the stage for the next act. Lord North told the Commons that he had not troubled to read the papers from the Congress.[24]

Peyton Randolph's Role

We come now to deal with intangibles and inferences, for which there is no definite proof, according to any works on the First Continental Congress that I have read. Did Randolph contribute anything significant to the First Continental Congress, or was he just a figurehead?

In what manner did Randolph influence the operation of the Congress? The Congress was normally in session daily from 9:00 until 3:00. Randolph was in the chair and did not participate in the debates. He denied no delegate his right to express his views, even at some length. After the day's session, the committees met and continued their labors as far into the evening as they deemed appropriate. Since Randolph was not on a committee, he was free until the next morning. He was the senior statesman at the Congress, as well as being its President, so he was invited everywhere to dinners and evening gatherings of delegates and influential Philadelphians. Within a week or so, he probably knew the political outlooks and personal temperaments of most of the delegates, from all colonies, and certainly better than anyone else in the Congress. As John J. Reardon, the primary biographer of Peyton Randolph, wrote: "From 3:00 in the afternoon until he retired in the evening, he was the voice of accommodation and continuity, achieving more through informal conversation and quiet consultation than many others accomplished in debate. A long leisurely dinner or a quiet evening of discussion over a glass of port was the context in which Randolph preferred to work. In these informal meetings, the delegates discovered that their President was the perfect politician—more concerned with the total problem than its several pieces and committed to steering Congress toward a statesmanlike response in this current crisis."[25]

The Congress included fifty-five delegates from twelve colonies. Forty-seven delegates had served in their own colonial legislature, and nine were, or had been, its Speaker. Half were lawyers, and most were prosperous by the standards of their own colony. Some colonies were Royal colonies, and some operated under special charters. Over the course of 150 years or so, different legislatures developed different rules of procedure, reflecting their different histories. As presiding officer, Randolph somehow created rules of procedure for the new Congress. I have seen no work that discussed what he did in this regard and how he did it, but it obviously was done and by him.

To consider the magnitude of Randolph's achievement, we must consider, first, the Virginia delegation, of which he was the head, and then the makeup of the Congress as a whole.

The Virginia delegation included Richard Henry Lee, who had brought on the audit of Speaker Robinson's accounts; Benjamin Harrison, whose friends were damaged in their finances and reputations by that audit; and Edmund Pendleton, who was Robinson's friend, protégé, lawyer, and executor. In addition, Lee was head of the Ohio Company; Harrison was an investor in its original competitor, the Loyal

Company (as was Randolph), and its later, and then current competitor, the Grand Ohio Company; and Pendleton was lawyer for the James River investors in both companies that competed with the Ohio Company. Washington was the leader of the 1754 veterans who were entitled to 200,000 acres, more than 10 percent of which he owned personally. Harrison was Randolph's brother-in-law; Harrison and Bland were his cousins and friends. Henry was a back-country demagogue lawyer, not really liked by most of the Virginia delegates, even by his political ally, Lee. On the other hand, Washington and Henry had jointly hired a surveyor during the summer of 1774 to survey some of their Western lands. Further, Washington had invited Henry to join him at Mount Vernon to ride together to Philadelphia. Pendleton had fallen in with Henry en route and unknowingly had made himself a third in their journey to the Congress. Washington had clearly planned to do some private visiting with Henry. Harrison and Pendleton were the delegates most seeking reconciliation. Bland, though a "conservative," wrote the first pamphlet to challenge the Ministry's authority in Virginia in 1766, and he had announced his intention to stand firm on the way to Philadelphia. Notwithstanding all these cross-currents, the Virginians were united in their belief that Virginia's constitutional rights were at stake and that the issue was of critical importance. Their unity on the critical issues was remarked by other delegates. Note how the Virginia delegation elected its three members to the two committees. Two were radicals and one was a conservative. Since the delegation was split three radicals, three conservatives and Randolph, it was Randolph's vote that determined the identity of the Virginia committee members. Of the Virginians, all but Henry and Pendleton dressed and lived particularly well. All of them brought their personal service slaves to Philadelphia and they had the air of command that slaveholding conferred. They had a degree of "swagger" that tended to overawe other delegates. While other delegations included members with legislative experience, every Virginian had been in the Burgesses for at least nine years, for Henry, and up to thirty-one years, for Bland. They were an impressive group. On the issue of allocation of voting strength, Harrison supported Henry, while Bland opposed him. While they parted on some issues, such as this, they held together on the critical issues. Even on the less critical issues, the minority would swing in behind the majority to present a solid front. Notably, Pendleton had set the precedent in Virginia earlier that year, when the courts were closed over his opposition. Randolph surely was an important factor in bringing about that solid front.

In the Congress as a whole, a large contingent sought reconciliation with Britain. The Pennsylvania delegation had personal reasons not shared with others, namely, their interests in Western land claims in opposition to the Virginians. The critical vote was the 6–5 vote tabling Galloway's proposal for a Grand Council in late September. The reconcilers and those persuaded by them, came within a hair of derailing the Congress altogether in late September. The 6–5 vote shows how narrow was the margin of support for any strong stand against Britain as of late September.

That the Congress as a whole came to so firm a stand against British abuse was no accident. Randolph, along with Lee, Harrison, and Bland arrived in Philadelphia three days early to allow them to politick, especially through Lee. That politicking resulted in Randolph's election as chairman and the strengthening of the Pennsylvania radicals by appointment of Thomson as Secretary and the selection of Carpenters' Hall as the venue for the Congress.

Most histories do not acknowledge the depth of division between the delegates and the narrowness of the decisive votes. On September 17, the Suffolk Resolves were "approved" with language that both the reconcilers and the radicals supported, since that language of support was so ambiguous. On September 18, Lee overreached the mood of the Congress, which was willing to approve training the militia, but not arming them. The mood of Congress changed with time. By the time of the vote on non-importation on September 26, Galloway recognized that he could not successfully defend against it and went with the rest. Then, on September 28, Galloway's proposal for a Grand Council was tabled, 6–5. By its votes on October 3 and October 6, revisiting the militia issue, and specifically approving Massachusetts' resistance, the Congress was ready to approve the use of force, unlike its position on the militia on September 18 and the Suffolk Resolves on September 17. By October 18, the Congress authorized local Committees (of Association or of Safety or of Inspection), independent of royal authority, a parallel government free from royal control. On October 22, Galloway's proposal was defeated.

In this summary, we can see how the mood of the Congress changed and stiffened against Britain. The effective date of that change can be pinpointed to sometime between late September and October 6, when the Congress had been in session for about four weeks, plus or minus a few days. What brought about the change? There was no outside event; no new outrage occurred in Massachusetts or elsewhere, and Boston's cry for help in the Suffolk Resolves had been finessed earlier. The arguments of the radicals changed few minds. The Massachusetts delegation were not trusted by many; if anything, they were blamed for the Tea Party that brought on the crisis. In the Virginia delegation, Henry had damaged his position on the Congress's first day, and Lee was unable to persuade the delegates to so obvious a measure as proposing that the colonies should see that their militias were adequately armed and adequately supplied with powder. I submit that a major cause of the change was Randolph's conversations with the delegates at nightly dinners and small gatherings over a glass of Port or Madeira. Randolph had foreseen the general trend of British policy from the time of the King's Speech in November 1768, and he was convinced that his personal safety, as well as Virginia's, was at stake. His earlier conclusions were confirmed by authorization of a Court of Inquiry in Rhode Island in 1772. Not that he ever would, or did, publicly verbalize that thought, but that was the direction in which he gently nudged the delegates.

The most obvious accomplishment of the Congress was the agreement on non-importation. The version finally adopted was a strict and absolute cessation of importation from Britain and Ireland and of most British West Indies products. Randolph and Virginia had experience with the non-importation agreement brought on by the Townshend Acts. The effort had been made to pick and choose, prohibiting some goods but not others. The result was confusion and difficulties of enforcement. Undoubtedly, these experiences were shared with other delegates and probably influenced the result.

For far-reaching effect, no action was as important as legitimizing the election by Associators of local Committees. Initially, their purpose was to enforce non-importation. But they eventually became the new governments of the colonies, since they were the elected bodies not under royal control. During the summer of 1774, this was the type of organization adopted in Virginia under Randolph's leadership as Moderator of the Association, then of the Convention of the Association. It surely is no accident that the Congress adopted the same type of organization that Randolph had created in Virginia. Again, we can detect Randolph's procedural genius. We can almost hear his quiet description of what Virginia had done, under his leadership, in one conversation group after another.

The principal obstacles, the leading reconcilers, were the majority of the Pennsylvania delegation, led by Joseph Galloway, their Speaker. John Dickinson, an early pamphleteer against Parliament's overreaching, was an investor in the Grand Ohio Company, but Galloway was both an investor and the front man for the main driving force behind the Grand Ohio Company, the Wharton brothers. Although the Board of Trade had ruled in early 1774 against the issuance of any new large land grants, such as that sought by the Grand Ohio Company, the Board of Trade was not the final authority in the British government. The Privy Council itself had blown hot and cold on the issue and might be influenced. Walpole and other powerful investors in Britain were working to change their positions. The incorporation into Quebec of all land north of the Ohio River defeated Virginia's claim to the area, and London now had the right to make a grant of many millions of acres to the Grand Ohio Company. But only if the colonies remained under British rule, such as under Galloway's proposed Grand Council subject to the authority of Parliament and the King. Indeed, Galloway failed to attend the Second Continental Congress, which convened in May 1775 after the fights at Lexington and Concord. Galloway joined General Gage and assisted his capture of Philadelphia. Dickinson refused to sign the Declaration of Independence but, nevertheless, went with his colony and continued to serve it. From the later actions of the two leaders of the Pennsylvania delegation, we may judge the conviction with which they favored reconciliation.

We come now to the dramatic moment in Philadelphia, in late

September, when it was learned that Virginia troops were in Fort Pitt, had seized the county seat of Pennsylvania's Westmoreland County, and had arrested three Pennsylvania magistrates for refusing to take an oath of allegiance to Virginia. Two of the three largest colonies, both members of the Congress, had committed acts of war against each other!

Sherlock Holmes commented about a similar remarkable event, namely, that "the dog did not bark." I have not found a single historian who mentions the reporting of this dangerous confrontation to the delegates and how they responded. The Pennsylvania reconcilers, whose colony had just been attacked, did not use this to undermine the influence of the Virginians, or, if they did, they gained no traction with their complaints or even obtained attention to them. How did this happen? Again, we can be sure that the matter was discussed with Randolph. One can guess that he calmly laid the blame on Lord Dunmore and attributed to Dunmore an intent to create dissension in the Congress. More than that would have been required. We can further guess that Randolph compared the boundary dispute between Virginia and Pennsylvania to other boundary disputes, most of which had been settled, and none of which had caused a colonial war. The old settlement between Pennsylvania and Maryland would have come to mind, as well as the recent settlement between Pennsylvania and New York, which Randolph had been involved in. There were also outstanding boundary disputes between New York and New Hampshire over Vermont and between New York and Connecticut regarding Western lands. Undoubtedly, the affair was represented as being blown out of proportion by Lord Dunmore. The dispute would not be settled for years. Were solutions discussed? Whatever Randolph's approach, he obviously soothed the delegates, even those from Pennsylvania. Did he, Lee, and Washington, and Pendleton and Harrison make private assurances of some sort to the Pennsylvanians? Did the Virginians, as a group, give some sort of private assurance? We will never know, but Virginia did relinquish its superior claim to the area around the forks of the Ohio, the Ohio Company grant was moved to Kentucky (and later lost in Richmond), and the settlers' grants were preserved.[26]

No dispute among the delegates over the frontier skirmish

between Virginia and Pennsylvania made its way into the historians' writings about the First Continental Congress. That is the remarkable fact. Yet, let us suppose that in November 1941 Germany had maneuvered Britain and the United States into a military confrontation over, say, Iceland, and that Britain had won that confrontation even while seeking a military alliance with the United States against Germany. That supposition is analogous to the one which actually occurred between Virginia and Pennsylvania. The dog did not bark. That was one of Randolph's greatest accomplishments at the Congress.

16

The Organization of Resistance and Coercion, September 1774–March 1775

In Virginia, Committees of Association, or Committees of Safety, began to be organized in June 1774, following the creation of a new Association on May 27 and its agreement to boycott the goods of the East India Company, more than two months before the August Convention agreed to non-importation of all goods but medicines as of November 1. By September and October 1774, Virginia committees were busy enforcing non-importation, even before the Congress approved it for all the colonies.[1] While the Congress agreed on non-importation to be effective as of December 1, 1774, Williamsburg did not elect a committee to ensure compliance until January 22, 1775. Randolph was elected chairman with Robert Carter Nicholas and eleven others. The only person of note not on the committee was John Randolph, the Attorney General.[2] By early 1775, Committees of Association had been organized in fifty-two Virginia counties. They were made up of a mixture of some old leaders and some new men. Their members totaled about 1,000 in Virginia and about 7,000 throughout the colonies.[3]

We should not believe that everyone, even in Virginia, much less in all colonies, enthusiastically supported non-importation and resistance to Britain. The committees were the machinery of intimidation. They oversaw merchants to prevent open importation and smuggling. But they also interrogated those with views "inimical to liberty" and compelled public apologies. Rather like the "new" Ku Klux Klan of the 1920s, they also set themselves up as enforcers of morals and the prohibitors of public extravagance and gambling.[4] To their credit, no mob was brought into the streets anywhere in Virginia. At Yorktown two half-chests of tea were destroyed, and both the London and local merchants were denounced.[5] Eleven hundred pounds of linens were seized and auctioned, and the proceeds were sent to relieve the poor of Boston. Clothing, bedding, and flour were also donated, or in some cases seized as being excessive, and transported to Boston.[6] Randolph regarded the committees as a legitimate means of self-government, despite their excesses. He urged that only "the gentlest measures" be used in bringing miscreants "to a sense of their misconduct." The committees should not exceed the powers given to them. "Rigorous methods" should be used only so "the public shall not suffer from obstinate opposition."[7]

Lord Dunmore reported to London in late December: "A Committee has been chosen in every county whose business it is to carry the Association of the Congress into execution, which Committee assumes an authority ... to watch the conduct of every inhabitant, without distinction, and ... to stigmatize, as they term it, such as they find transgressing what they are now hardy enough to call the Laws of the Congress ... [by] inviting the vengeance of an outrageous and lawless mob to be exercised upon the unhappy victims."[8]

In January 1775, urged on by Washington and Mason, the Fairfax County Committee ordered all able-bodied men to serve in the militia. They levied a tax to purchase ammunition and ordered the sheriff to collect it. The Fairfax County Committee obviously had undertaken to act as the County Court.[9] They undoubtedly were not alone. As we have seen, about this time Governor Dunmore wrote that not a Justice of the Peace acted in Virginia except as a Committee man.

As fall became winter that 1774–1775, the colonies received news of the response in Britain to the Congress's carefully worded petition to the Crown and to the people of Britain. In October, the King forbade export of arms and ammunition from Britain to the colonies and ordered the Governors and naval officers in colonial waters to prevent their importation from elsewhere. A new Parliament was elected and returned Lord North to power.[10] A Massachusetts congress met in October–December 1774 and constituted itself a rebel government.

The new Parliament met and received the King's Speech from the Throne on November 29, 1774. King George III condemned "violence of a very criminal nature in Massachusetts." "You may depend on my firm and steadfast resolution to withstand every attempt to weaken or impair the supreme authority of this Legislature over all the dominions of my Crown."[11] A motion to obtain the Ministry's American papers before endorsing the King's attack on the colonies, was defeated 264–73.[12] The King was known to have stated publicly, "We must master them or totally leave them to themselves and treat them as aliens."[13] On January 19, 1775, Lord North laid Congress's proceedings before Parliament. On January 29, Lord Chatham (Pitt) proposed in the Lords the withdrawal of troops from Boston. It was defeated 18–68.[14] On February 1, Chatham proposed the repeal of all repressive Acts and that no tax be levied by Parliament without the consent of the colonial Assemblies, in exchange for a joint Congress's granting the King perpetual revenue. This attempt to resolve the issue of revenues was also defeated 61–32.[15] On January 23, 1775, a petition by London merchants for "healing remedies" was defeated 197–81.[16] On February 2, 1775, Parliament acceded to Lord North's suggestion and declared Massachusetts to be in rebellion, encouraged by illegal combinations in several other (unnamed) colonies. Parliament asked the King to enforce "due obedience" to the laws and authority of Parliament.[17] Transportation for treason, hanging, drawing, and quartering were genuine threats to many colonial leaders. In order to further cripple New England, on February 10, 1775, Parliament passed the "Fish Bill," which prohibited their access to the North Atlantic fisheries, most notably, the Grand Banks, and prohibited their trade with anyone but Britain, Ireland, and the British West Indies.[18] As if closing the Port of Boston had not been enough! With these actions of the King and Parliament, the colonies really were left only the choice of submission or revolution, although, even at this point, many continued to seek "reconciliation."

It appears clear that Randolph's belief at this point in time was that revolution was unavoidable. He had been instrumental in having the Congress create the local Committees, the machinery of independent government throughout the colonies, modeled on that created first in Virginia, probably of his own idea. He himself was chairman of the

Committee in Virginia's capital. He knew of, and obviously approved of, these committees having undertaken the functions of government at the local level, even that of raising taxes for defense. While he sought to ameliorate the excesses of some of these committees, he supported their legitimacy. When he called for the next meeting of the Convention, he had it meet in Richmond, out of reach of both the Governor and the British warships at Yorktown.

The Second Convention, March 20, 1775

Virginia Is Placed in a "Posture of Defense" by Three Votes

On January 19, 1775, Randolph issued a call for a Second Convention of the Association to convene in Richmond on March 20 to elect delegates to the Second Continental Congress and "for other purposes of public security."[1] The August 1774 Convention had authorized him, as Moderator, to reconvene the Association if he deemed it necessary. Randolph added a new element. He requested that the delegates to the Convention be selected in new elections. He probably consulted the Committee of Correspondence before assuming this enlarged authority; its approval would bind the Burgesses as a practical matter.[2] The designation of Richmond, a village of 600, was also a new feature; the August 1774 Convention had been held in Williamsburg. Randolph obviously felt the need for greater security than that offered by the capital with the port at Yorktown only thirteen miles away. The news of the King's Speech on November 29, 1774, indicated that the members of the Convention might be at risk. Almost every county and other constituency sent at least two delegates. The College of William and Mary did not participate; their delegate was John Randolph, who opposed the Convention.[3]

Randolph opened the Second Convention in St. John's Church with the formalities that Governors had previously used in opening the General Assembly. He urged the Convention to "proceed in the deliberation and discussions of the several important matters which should come before them, with that prudence, decency and order *which has distinguished their conduct on all former occasions*" (emphasis supplied). Randolph thereby treated the Convention as a new de facto legislature. Undoubtedly, by pre-arrangement with Randolph, the Convention was moved to adopt "the same rules and orders as are

St. John's Episcopal Church, exterior, Richmond, Virginia (Colonial Williamsburg Foundation, No. 1977-248-2).

established in the House of Burgesses." Randolph's title was changed from "Moderator" to "President," indicating a more permanent position. The Convention had thereby accepted Randolph's implied invitation for it to constitute itself as a de facto legislature.[4]

Randolph, as chairman of Virginia's delegation to the First Continental Congress, placed before the Convention the proceedings of the Congress. In addition, he gave an oral report. He said he had received a report that "we are to be treated as rebels and enemies without any ceremony." He had another report that "we might hope for repeal of the new Acts if we pay for the tea and acknowledge the superiority of Parliament." "Superiority" would have to be properly defined; otherwise Virginia and the other colonies would need to pursue their plan of non-importation.[5] The entire proceedings of the Congress were approved on March 21.[6]

On March 23, Patrick Henry rose to move that Virginia be placed in a posture of defense and that "a committee draft a plan for embody-

St. John's Episcopal Church, interior, Richmond, Virginia (Colonial Williamsburg Foundation, No. 1990-2192).

ing, arming and disciplining" a militia, since the old militia law had expired. Richard Henry Lee seconded. Henry described Virginia's condition as being virtually in arms. The County Committees had become its de facto government. The Convention could either allow the colony to fragment or take steps to unify it.[7] Pendleton objected that this would mean that the Convention was acting as a government. Pendleton, Bland, and Harrison argued that the time to arm had not arrived. Robert Carter Nicholas said the resolution went too far; he wanted Britain's errors rectified without altering the constitution. Pendleton predicted that Britain would neither repeal the Acts nor resort to force, but rather that they faced a long, drawn-out commercial struggle.[8] Lee and Jefferson supported Henry's motion. Thomas Nelson, Jr., of Yorktown shocked the "conservatives" by supporting Henry's motion.

Henry's reply comes ringing down the years. He began slowly. We must face the truth. There was no longer any hope for reform, referring to "the illusions of hope." He reviewed at length the course of the dispute with Britain, the failures of petitions, the increasingly violent and arrogant statements of the Ministry and Crown and Britain's growing military power in the colonies. "Gentlemen may cry peace, peace, but there is no peace." Before long, "the clash of resounding arms" would come from Boston. War was inevitable. "Let it come.... What is it that these gentlemen wish? Is life so dear, or peace so sweet, as to be purchased at the price of chains and slavery? Forbid it, Almighty God! I know not what course others may take, but, as for me—give me liberty or give me death!"[9]

Henry's motion passed by only five votes in a Convention of 107 or more.[10]

Randolph appointed a committee of twelve to produce a militia plan to put Virginia in a posture of defense. He appointed Henry as chairman; R. H. Lee; Jefferson; Colonels Washington, Andrew Lewis (militia commander of the 1774 victory at Point Pleasant), Adam Smith, and William Christian, leading supporters of Henry; and, as minority members, Pendleton, Nicholas, and Harrison.[11] The committee plan called for musters of "independent" militia in each county and recommended that the county Association committees "form one or more companies of infantry and troop of horse, to be in constant training and readiness to act on any emergency" and collect from their constituents money to buy one-half pound of gunpowder, one pound of lead, flints, and cartridge paper for every tithable person in the county.[12] A central committee would act as purchasing agent for counties that wanted one. The conservatives wanted to delete the portion about raising money, arguing that the Convention should say that it was only their opinion that this should be done, so as not to assume governmental powers. Henry responded that the way to solve their objection was for the Convention officially to constitute itself a government. At this threat, knowing now that Henry had the votes to do so, the conservatives backed down. The committee's plan was then approved unanimously.[13]

The Convention also appointed a committee to encourage arts and manufactures. The Convention recommended that lawyers, litigants, and witnesses not attend the General Court and that County Courts hear only attachment proceedings.[14]

Considering the need for Pennsylvania's participation in the resistance to British coercion, it is notable that the Convention also passed a resolution thanking Governor Dunmore for his "truly noble, wise and spirited Conduct" in the Western campaign the preceding year, while the Congress was meeting.[15] Since a new Pennsylvania delegation to the Second Congress had not yet appeared on the scene, this resolution might be taken as a heavily veiled threat to the Pennsylvania reconcilers.

Finally, the Convention elected Randolph as Chairman of the delegation to the Second Continental Congress (107 votes), along with Washington (106), Henry (105), Lee (103), Pendleton (100), Harrison (94), and Bland (90). The delegates indicated their concern for Randolph's health by electing Jefferson as his "alternate."[16]

Randolph's intentions are clearly disclosed. The May 27, 1774, Association and the August 1774 Convention members were overwhelmingly Burgesses elected before the crisis had arisen. Randolph called for a new election of delegates by the County Committees of the Association. Those who opposed the Association and the non-importation agreement would be less likely to vote or stand for election than they would in a county election for Burgesses. (The absence of John Randolph is the most prominent of these.) He thereby obtained a Convention that would probably be more radical than the House of Burgesses itself, even though the leading Members on both sides were returned. A new poll given with the crisis in view would also have greater legitimacy in dealing with that crisis. Indeed, about one-fourth of the delegates had not served in the Burgesses or the August 1774 Convention.[17]

Randolph's intentions are also clearly evidenced by his opening the Convention with many of the formalities of a new House of Burgesses. He had obviously conferred with Henry, so that the Convention took steps, such as adoption of the House of Burgesses' rules, which brought it to the very edge of constituting itself a successor government to the General Assembly, the ultimate revolutionary act.

Randolph remarked, in presenting the proceedings of the Congress, that "we" were to be treated as rebels by Britain. Randolph knew of the lopsided vote for a Parliament that continued Lord North's Ministry in power and the King's November 1774 Speech from the Throne condemning Massachusetts and other unnamed colonies and reiterating his determination to enforce Parliament's authority over the colonies. By March 20, he may or may not have had news of the January votes in Parliament against any form of compromise, but he already had the tone of the new Commons in its voting down, 264–72, the resolution to examine the Ministry's records before considering the King's and Ministry's program to reduce the colonies to submission. Randolph correctly read the signs; there would be no compromise this time.

That being so, Randolph, like Henry, had concluded that there would be a war. He and the other colonial leaders were already rebels and were personally at great risk. He clearly had conferred with Henry in advance of saying that "we" are rebels. The militia plan presented by Henry's committee had been drafted in advance by Jefferson, and Henry and Randolph had probably discussed the essential contents of the plan. The meshing of Randolph's actions and those of Henry conclusively prove the collaboration between them during this Convention.

March 23 was the critical moment. Even with the election of the most favorable body possible, the weight of experienced, highly respected leaders against Henry's motion was impressive. Voting against Henry were three of the delegates to the First Continental Congress, Edmund Pendleton, Benjamin Harrison, and Richard Bland; the Treasurer of the Colony, Robert Carter Nicholas; the leading expert on constitutional history and law in Virginia, Richard Bland; and the leading courthouse lawyer in Virginia, Edmund Pendleton. The vote was unbelievably close——a five-vote majority in a Convention of at least 107 members, which could have gone the other way by changing only three votes. Pendleton's crystal ball into the future—a prolonged commercial struggle without the use of military force—was way off the mark. Henry's forecast was dead on: Lexington and Concord were less than a month away. Virginia came within the margin of three voters in the Convention to not having organized and financed its militia in advance of that event.

There can be no doubt that Randolph did everything his long experience had prepared him to do to bring about this result and, as in Williamsburg and in Philadelphia, that he had visited quietly with the delegates that he thought he might persuade. He correctly counted his votes, but it was still as close as it could be. But for Randolph's placing his own thumb on the scale, the vote undoubtedly would have gone the other way. By approving the militia bill, the Convention had picked up the reins to pull the County Committees together and became, in effect, a parallel government in Virginia. While Virginia's leaders were united in their belief that Britain had violated their rights, they were closely divided as to the response to be made. The delegations to both Continental Congresses mirrored that close division, four to three. If the conservatives had won this critical vote, in the manner of legislative bodies, they would have won succeeding votes by larger margins. The most important vote taken after the militia resolution was the decision to elect Thomas Jefferson as an alternate for Randolph. It is important to emphasize that the leaders of the conservatives had again demonstrated their loyalty to Virginia and their dedication to its unity and safety. After losing the militia vote so closely, they had closed ranks and approved the militia committee's plan unanimously.

Those who minimize Randolph's importance and influence in the creation of this nation, as having been too cautious and not having led on the way toward independence, should look again at this Convention and the March 23 vote.

18

Dunmore's Response
Land Titles and Gunpowder

After Governor Dunmore's victorious return to Williamsburg in late October or early November 1774, he had ample time to review the actions of the First Continental Congress, which had adjourned on October 26. As the Virginia County Committees organized themselves to enforce non-importation, effective December 1, this vigorous servant of the Crown obviously had time to communicate with London, though I have found no mention of that correspondence.

Dunmore sought to intimidate the 1754 veterans who had received their land grants in 1772 or 1773, and those who had purchased their grants. Word was spread among the frontier settlements that their titles were questioned and could be voided. Washington first heard this rumor after his arrival home on March 31 from the Second Convention. One of the officer-grantees told Washington that Dunmore had questioned whether the surveyor, retained by Washington for the grantees, had been qualified under the statute. Washington wrote Dunmore, outlining the history of the grants and showing how the legal requirements had been met. He wrote that he would not trouble the Governor but for the importunities of grantees disturbed by rumors. He asked to know the facts and offered to take any further steps Dunmore required. On April 18, 1775, Dunmore coldly wrote Washington that he had a report that the surveyor was not legally qualified. If that were the case, the grants were void. By holding the issue open, did the Governor expect to intimidate the grantees, including Washington who had 23,000 acres at risk, to have them support the Crown or lose their grants? Or did his threat cause the grantees to conclude that the

147

18. Dunmore's Response

preservation of their grants necessitated the termination of Britain's control over the colonies? In either case, the timing of Dunmore's letter to Washington is significant. Although Dunmore's position was not known in Richmond before the Second Convention adjourned on March 27, news of it reached Washington in early April. It undoubtedly was known to Randolph when the next crisis arose.[1]

British warships were not normally anchored at Yorktown. At least two naval vessels, the armed schooner *Magdalen* and the man-of-war H.M.S. *Fowey*, were present at Yorktown on April 19, 1775. I have not seen any mention of when they arrived and how long they stayed. H.M.S. *Fowey* was still at Yorktown on June 9, to which Governor Dunmore fled during the General Assembly. It is likely that one of them brought Dunmore orders to seize the powder at Williamsburg. It is not known whether the naval presence at Yorktown was continuous during these weeks.

On the night of April 20–21, 1775, a detachment of fifteen marines from the *Magdalen* disembarked at Yorktown and marched to Williamsburg. The Governor had a key to the Colony's Magazine, which he provided for the marines, along with one of his personal wagons. About 3:00 a.m. they entered the Magazine and loaded the wagon with twenty barrels of powder, the great majority of the powder stored, and transported it to H.M.S. *Fowey*, which had moved to the James River in order to avoid a return by the same route.[2]

Upon discovery of this on the morning of April 21, an angry crowd, armed and beating drums, assembled near the Capitol, threatening to storm the Palace. Randolph, Robert Carter Nicholas, and several "gentlemen" intervened and proposed that the municipal government should handle the matter. They prepared a strongly worded protest, which Nicholas and Randolph, in his capacity as Recorder, presented to the Governor. They found that Dunmore had armed his household and several naval officers with him.

Dunmore assured them on his honor that the powder was taken

due to rumors of a planned slave rebellion nearby, and that it was removed at night to avoid alarming the populace but could be promptly returned if needed. When this was reported to the crowd, they did not believe Dunmore. Randolph never said whether he believed it. Randolph and others persuaded the crowd that nothing could be gained by violence and they should disperse.[3]

Riders went out to summon militia to assemble at Fredericksburg. By April 27, 600 militia had gathered there. Randolph wrote to ask them to wait, telling them that Dunmore had given private assurance that he would return the powder. Dunmore's honor was at stake. Randolph wrote, "He thinks he acted for the best and will not be compelled to do what we have abundant reason to believe he would cheerfully do, were he left to himself." Randolph thanked the militia but asked that "matters be quieted for the present at least. Violent measures may produce effects, which God only knows the consequences of."[4]

Dunmore had brought a number of marines and sailors from the ships to defend the Palace. If they were attacked, he threatened to free the slaves and burn the entire town.[5]

Peyton and Betty Randolph, together with Benjamin Harrison, left Williamsburg on April 28 to travel to Philadelphia for the new Congress due to convene on May 10. They spent the first night at Pendleton's home. Since Dunmore had pronounced the Congress "unwarrantable," they accepted the offer of a military escort to the Potomac.[6]

On April 29, the *Williamsburg Gazette* published news of the April 19 fights at Lexington and Concord. The British troops had marched to Lexington and Concord to seize powder and other military goods supposedly stored in Concord and to arrest Massachusetts' radical leaders. They failed in their mission and started a war. The connection between movements of British forces to seize military stores on essentially the same day, April 19 and April 20 in the two leading dissident colonies several hundred miles apart, was obvious to all. It was immediately apparent that Dunmore had lied to Randolph and Nicholas.[7]

Also on April 29, news of Lexington and Concord was received by over 1,000 militia gathered at Fredericksburg. While other militia units debated what to do, Henry was elected leader of about 100 volunteers from his home County of Hanover. The night of May 2, Henry secretly dispatched a dozen men to surround the plantation home of Richard Corbin, the King's Receiver General of the Colony's quit rents paid to the Crown. They were to demand payment for the powder from the King's funds and to arrest Corbin, if he refused. The next morning Henry led the rest of the volunteers toward Williamsburg, adding individuals and units as they progressed. Henry's intent was to enforce payment for the powder, since the powder itself was out of reach. Henry sent a messenger to Nicholas, the Treasurer, to ask him to calculate the cost of the powder. H.M.S. *Fowey* meanwhile had returned to Yorktown.[8]

That same morning, Dunmore convened the Council, made up of Thomas Nelson, Jr., president of the Council; the Rev. John Camm; Ralph Wormeley; Richard Corbin, the Receiver; Gawin Corbin; William Byrd III of Westover; and John Page. Page was the only one to challenge the Governor's seizure of the powder; all the rest remained silent. The Council and Governor issued a proclamation "denouncing the rapid recurrence to arms" and defiance of executive authority.[9]

Corbin had spent the night in town. The men sent to his home missed him, but their purpose had been communicated to him. The night of May 3, while bivouacked a dozen miles from Williamsburg, Henry received bills of exchange from Corbin totaling £330, the value set by Nicholas. Henry demanded endorsement by a known Whig, since he said he otherwise did not trust that the bills would not be contested upon presentation in London. This distrust pointedly included Carter Braxton, who had tried to persuade Henry not to march on Williamsburg and later had offered to endorse the bills. Braxton, who had brought the bills from Corbin to Henry, then returned to Williamsburg with Henry's message. Meanwhile, Dunmore had drawn up cannon in front of the Palace and given notice that, if Henry's militia entered Williamsburg, he would order the ships to shell Yorktown until it was reduced to ashes. Thomas Nelson, Jr., president of the Council and a resident of Yorktown, rode out with Braxton early the next morning in time to halt Henry's march toward the capital. Henry accepted Nelson's endorsement of Corbin's bills of exchange and receipted for the payment on behalf of Virginia's delegates to the

Congress to be used to purchase powder. The crisis had passed. The militia returned home, and Henry left late for Philadelphia on May 11.[10] Dunmore soon after denounced Henry as a rebel.

It has been easy to contrast the heroic and successful role played by Henry with the cautious, or even purportedly gullible role played by Randolph. Were Randolph and Nicholas actually so gullible as to believe Dunmore's assurances? That seems hardly likely; the general belief was that Dunmore was lying. Randolph was careful to say what Dunmore had told them without ever vouching for Dunmore's truthfulness, though his message to the militia that "we have abundant reason to believe" that Dunmore would return the powder comes close to doing so. True, if he were unwillingly acting under orders. The events proved that Randolph was correct in saying that, if Dunmore's hand were called, the consequences likely would be terrible.

Randolph was en route to Philadelphia when he received the news of Lexington and Concord, which cast Dunmore's seizure of the powder as one part of a concerted effort by Britain to disarm the leading dissident colonies. Henry was in a position to act on that information, but Randolph was not. His position in the Congress would serve Virginia's interests as well as those of the other colonies. The singling out of Massachusetts and Virginia as the targets for disarming and the attempt to arrest the radical leaders of Massachusetts made it apparent that the leaders in Virginia would also be targets for arrest and transportation for trial for treason.

It is clear that Randolph concluded, correctly, that the pow-

Carter Braxton, **by an unidentified artist, watercolor on ivory, c. 1775 (National Portrait Gallery, Smithsonian Institution. No. NPG.98.33).**

der was gone and had been placed beyond the Virginians' reach. To trigger Dunmore's destruction of the colony's capital would not restore the gunpowder. Without the news of Lexington and Concord, there was no absolute proof from which to label Dunmore's soothing assurances as lies. Henry had that proof when he marched on Williamsburg; Randolph did not when he left for Philadelphia. That being the case, Randolph did well when he calmed both the townspeople and the militia in order to preserve Williamsburg.

19

The Second Continental Congress, May 10, 1775

Peyton and Betty Randolph and Harrison spent the first night of their trip to Philadelphia at Edmund Pendleton's home and then traveled together with him. Since the news of Lexington and Concord reached Fredericksburg and Williamsburg on April 29, they probably received it on the same day or the next as they drove north. They accepted a military guard to the Potomac. Randolph, Lee, Washington, Bland, Pendleton, and Harrison arrived timely; Henry arrived late, having delayed to enforce payment for the gunpowder.

The makeup of some delegations had changed. While most of the Pennsylvania delegates were returned, Joseph Galloway, their chairman and Speaker of their legislature, had declared himself a Tory and declined to return to the Congress. Benjamin Franklin had returned from London and joined the delegation. The control of the Pennsylvania legislature had shifted, so the Second Continental Congress convened in the State House instead of Carpenter's Hall. In New York also, the Tories had lost control of the legislature, and their delegation had also changed.[1] Virginia's delegation again was unusual. Every member was a man of property as well as position. Pendleton and Henry were "new men," but they had succeeded in acquiring substantial estates. The same could not be said of many other delegations.[2] The Virginians contrasted markedly from the Massachusetts delegation, led by a radical revolutionary politician, Samuel Adams, who was impecunious.

The Second Continental Congress convened on the date set, May 10, 1775.[3] Randolph was elected President of the new Congress.[4]

154

Britain's armed aggression at Lexington and Concord on April 19 had created a sense of urgency. That sense was reflected in the fact that the Congress sat as a Committee of the Whole for most of the time from May 11–26, facilitating a more expeditious dispatch of its business.[5] By the time the Congress convened on May 10, New England militia had hemmed the British garrison in Boston. Only days later, word was received that Ethan Allen and Benedict Arnold had captured the key to Lake Champlain, Fort Ticonderoga, on May 10 and with it, large quantities of cannon and munitions. The door to Canada up Lake Champlain had been opened for the colonials and closed to the British.[6]

At its outset, the Congress heard reports received by different colonies from their London agents. They uniformly reported the unsatisfactory response of the Ministry to petitions from many colonies and the indifference to colonial grievances. Franklin himself had been Pennsylvania's agent.

Dickinson of Pennsylvania and Pendleton advocated a new petition to the King.[7] Other delegates advocated mobilization. On May 21, Pendleton embraced a policy of both a petition and mobilization as a compromise. While the course of action was being considered, reports arrived from Virginia that Dunmore had summoned the General Assembly to convene on June 1. It was also reported that Dunmore intended to arm the slaves.[8] Randolph resigned as President on May 24, and he and Betty immediately set out for Williamsburg. Bland also left for Williamsburg. Middleton of South Carolina declined to serve again as a temporary President, due to poor health. Sam Adams and John Adams nominated John Hancock of Massachusetts in the belief that he would resign when Randolph returned.[9] On May 26, after Randolph's departure, Pendleton's compromise was approved to pursue petition for reconciliation and mobilization simultaneously.[10]

On February 20, Lord North had laid before the Commons a plan for reconciliation. Parliament passed a resolution on February 27 that "any colony that contributed to the common defense and provided support for the civil government and the administration of justice … would be relieved of paying taxes or duties except those necessary for the regulation of commerce."[11] There was no indication of the amount of the "pro rata" contribution that would be required, and there was no offer to suspend or repeal the Intolerable Acts. The context of this "Conciliatory Resolution" was that North's Ministry had just defeated Pitt's resolutions to recognize colonial self-government and to withdraw troops from Boston and had passed the Fish Bill. Edmund Burke stated in the Commons that "Lord North plainly told us he was convinced the colonies would not accept it."[12] The "Conciliatory Resolution" was sent to each colony individually, pointing up its true intent to divide the colonies.

The Congress received a copy of Parliament's Conciliatory Resolution on May 26, the same day it voted to proceed on both tracks. The delegates obviously saw through its real intent, as indicated by the selection of John Adams, Lee, Jefferson, and Franklin to draft a reply. The time for reconciliation had evidently passed. In Randolph's absence, between June 10–16, the Congress authorized a regular army of 15,000 men, two-thirds to be sent to Massachusetts and one-third to New York, and adopted Articles of War (the code of military justice). On June 15, Washington was elected Commander-in-Chief and soon left for Army headquarters at Cambridge, Massachusetts, arriving there on July 2. On June 22, the Congress authorized issuance of $2,000,000 in paper money to finance the Army.[13]

Though Randolph was no longer in Philadelphia, it was important that he be kept advised of the actions of the Congress. As Speaker of the Burgesses, his intelligence needed to be better than Dunmore's while events unfolded so rapidly in Williamsburg. The Committees of Correspondence performed such a function. We have seen how rapidly the Committee in Boston communicated with its delegation in Philadelphia, on one occasion through Paul Revere. There is every reason to believe that Randolph arranged for rapid communication from Philadelphia.

20

The Last General Assembly, June 1, 1775

Peyton and Betty Randolph, presumably accompanied by Bland, left Philadelphia by coach on May 24 or 25 and traveled rapidly to Williamsburg so that he would be present when the General Assembly convened on June 1. They arrived on May 30, and Randolph was given a militia guard.[1] They had six or seven days to travel about 300 miles with the stress of a highly charged session at the end of the road. Considering that the Richmond Convention had been so concerned for Randolph's health that they had sent Jefferson as his alternate, it must have been a particularly hard trip.

Randolph was elected Speaker on June 1. He appointed a committee to inspect the Magazine and report on the loss of gunpowder. The House unanimously approved the actions of the First Continental Congress.[2] The Richmond Convention had already done so, but the approval of the Burgesses would have soothed questions of legality by some conservatives.

The general tone in Williamsburg was so hostile to Britain that, faced with being held responsible for the gunpowder seizure, Governor Dunmore and his family fled to a warship at Yorktown, the *Fowey* on June 9. John Randolph, as Attorney General, was the highest-ranking Royal officer in the colony after the Governor's flight. He was also the delegate from the College of William and Mary. He appointed himself as intermediary between Dunmore and the House and made several trips between Williamsburg and the *Fowey*. The gap was unbridgeable, and John Randolph's efforts were in vain.[3] Events overtook the Governor and the Burgesses. Word was received of a major battle at

20. The Last General Assembly, June 1, 1775

Bunker's Hill, across the Charles River from Boston, in which the colonials acquitted themselves admirably and inflicted heavy losses on the British regulars.[4]

On June 12, the Burgesses rejected Parliament's Conciliatory Resolution. On June 23, Randolph convened the citizens of Williamsburg at the Court House and asked them to station militia in the capital to guard against a surprise attack by Dunmore. This was his first public acknowledgment that a state of rebellion existed. On June 24, the Burgesses adjourned. This proved to be the last regular session of the House of Burgesses. Subsequent efforts to convene the House failed for lack of a quorum. On June 26, Randolph, acting as President of the Convention, issued a call for the Third Convention to meet at Richmond on July 17.[5]

In March and April, Randolph had presided over the Second Convention in Richmond. He had set up the Richmond Convention as being almost the government of Virginia. After the Richmond Convention, he took less than a week's rest in Williamsburg before setting out for Philadelphia for the Second Continental Congress. There he had presided over the Second Continental Congress and left with only travel time to Williamsburg. He had only a day to recover from the rapid trip from Philadelphia to Williamsburg, while conferring and preparing to preside over the House of Burgesses commencing on June 1. He managed the Burgesses for three and a half weeks as it wound down.

Note that none of the routine business of government was done. The entire effort dealt with approving the actions of the First Continental Congress, replying to Parliament's Conciliatory Resolution by refusing to take its bait, and confronting Dunmore over his seizure of the colony's gunpowder. Note the actions of the First Continental Congress were approved unanimously. Unity was astonishing, considering what Virginia was about to do in challenging the world's greatest power. The Burgesses were not called upon to ratify the actions of the Second Convention nor to ratify the Convention's election of delegates to the Second Continental Congress. Recall that the May 1774 Burgesses had been dissolved before it could address the Intolerable Acts. The delegates to the First Continental Congress had been elected by the August 1774 Convention in Williamsburg, and the delegates to the Second

Continental Congress had been elected by the Second Convention held in Richmond in March 1775. The House implicitly recognized that the legislation to prepare for war had been done by the Convention and was legitimate.

John Randolph did not resign his position as Attorney General; it simply dissolved as the bonds with Britain parted. He lost a salary of £340 a year as Attorney General.[6] In late August, John Randolph conveyed all his property in Virginia to Peyton Randolph, John Blair, Jr., and James Cocke with instructions to sell it, pay his debts, and send the balance to him in England. On August 25, John Randolph published an announcement in the *Virginia Gazette* that he intended to leave Virginia for a few months and had appointed Peyton Randolph, Blair, and Cocke as his legal agents and referred all business as Attorney General to Blair. On September 8, John, his wife, and two daughters—all his family except his son, Edmund—left Williamsburg for Norfolk to embark for England, never to return.[7] Edmund obtained an appointment to Washington's staff as an aide-de-camp, supported by recommendations from his uncle, Benjamin Harrison, and from Richard Henry Lee, whose letter to Washington was cosigned by Henry and Jefferson. He later served as Governor of Virginia and as Attorney General in Washington's first Presidential administration.

Randolph's immediate family suffered worse division in the Revolution than any other family in Virginia. His sister, Mary Grymes, and her husband, Philip Grymes, had both died in 1768. Their only surviving son, John Randolph Grymes, left for England, though he did return after the Revolution.[8]

A handful of other prominent men in Virginia became Tories. William Byrd III, a member of the Council, deeply in debt, disinherited his son for siding with the Revolutionaries, and shot himself on January 1, 1777.[9] Richard Corbin, a member of the Council and also Receiver General, retired to his plantation and sat out the war. Councilor Ralph Wormeley also left for England. After the Treaty of Paris in 1783, under which Tories were entitled to recover compensation for confiscated property, only between thirteen (Tate) and twenty-four (Knollenberg) Tories born in Virginia filed claims.[10]

Thirteen to twenty-four claims filed by natives of the most populous colony in British North America! This figure, alone, demonstrates Randolph's success in holding Virginia together. But when considered in contrast with the experience of the other colonies, either "thirteen" or "twenty-four" appears to be miraculous. The white population of Massachusetts was about the same as the white population of Virginia. Two hundred three native-born from Massachusetts filed claims, eight to fifteen times the number from Virginia. Over 1,000 Tories were evacuated from Boston with the British garrison in 1776. I have seen no specific numbers for those who fled from Charleston with the British evacuation in 1783 nor the total who settled in the West Indies. However, 10,000 whites and slaves settled in Jamaica alone, and many went to other British islands in the West Indies. The most phenomenal evacuation was that from New York City and Long Island in 1783. Thirty-two thousand Tories had to be evacuated before the British troops would leave. The demand on shipping was so great that the British were several months late in delivering up New York as required by the Treaty of Paris, but they would not leave until the Loyalists were safely embarked.[11] These massive evacuations were only part of the picture. They take no account of the numbers of those who fled singly, in family groups or in small groups to friendly territory. New Englanders and upstate New Yorkers trekked to Canada. Three thousand Philadelphians and other Pennsylvanians who enthusiastically welcomed the British troops in 1777, and collaborated with them during the occupation, embarked down the Delaware River when the troops left. Carolinians and Georgians went to British territories in East Florida and West Florida. Wherever British ships approached the shore during the war, they offered a haven for Tories along the coast. Some crossed the mountains and took the Ohio and Mississippi Rivers to New Orleans, especially during the years before the Spanish entered the war against Britain. In parts of the colonies, Tories were found in large enough numbers to create Loyalist companies or even regiments. At the battle of King's Mountain on the border of North and South Carolina, the turning point of Cornwallis's campaign in the Carolinas and Georgia, the only King's soldier born outside the colonies was Major Ferguson, their commander. There were no such organized bodies of Loyalist Virginia troops.

The Third Convention, Richmond, July 17, 1775

On July 17, 1775, the Third Virginia Convention convened in Richmond. Randolph was in the chair as President. He was exhausted by his travels and constant service in Richmond, Philadelphia, and Williamsburg beginning with the March Convention. His legs were badly swollen, and he was feeble, but he handled matters as chairman reasonably well. When the Convention went into a Committee of the Whole, Richard Bland was in the chair. His health also was deteriorating, presaging his death the next year, and he declined reelection to the Congress. He could hardly see, and progress was very slow. Robert Carter Nicholas was chairman of the principal committee. He began to assume Bland's duties as Bland proved unable to perform them. Pendleton, Harrison, Henry, and Jefferson joined the Convention on August 9 during the Congress's recess from August 2 to September 5. On August 16, the Convention unanimously recommended that Randolph should retire to rest before the reconvening of the Congress. Nicholas was then elected President pro tem during Randolph's absence, and Harrison presided over the Committee of the Whole. Peyton and Betty Randolph returned to Williamsburg until their departure for Philadelphia on August 27.[1]

The Convention labored slowly to create the necessary organization for revolution. For three weeks, there was much talk in the Committee of the Whole but little action. The first vote of consequence was the election on August 5 of Henry as commander of the First Virginia Regiment and Commander-in-Chief of Virginia troops. He won a narrow victory over Hugh Mercer, even though he was not present yet at the Convention. On August 8, Nicholas, instead of Bland, presented an ordnance for "raising a force for defense of the colony."[2] The pace quickened after the return of the four Congressional delegates on August 9.

On August 11, new delegates to the Congress were elected, since Washington had gone to Boston and Henry had accepted the military command. The new delegation was Randolph (89 votes), Richard Henry Lee (88), Jefferson (85), Harrison (82), Thomas Nelson, Jr. (66), Bland (61), and George Wythe (58).[3] Pendleton had declined to run for reasons of health. The makeup of the delegation, again, was three radicals, three conservatives, and Randolph. After his election, Bland declined to accept due to age.

The vacancy created by Bland's declining the seat was filled by election of Frank Lee over Carter Braxton by a margin of one vote.[4] The makeup of the delegation was thus four radicals, two conservatives and Randolph. Considering Randolph's health, this was a critical vote; otherwise, upon his incapacitation, the Virginia vote would have been split, three to three.

By this time the Committee of the Whole had shaped its proposed ordinances for consideration by the Convention. A Committee of Safety was elected on August 16 as the Convention's executive. It included Pendleton as President (77 votes), George Mason (72), John Page (70), Bland (66), Thomas Ludwell Lee (63), Paul Carrington (54), Dudley Digges (41), William Cabell (39), James Mercer (38), Carter Braxton (38) and John Tabb (36).[5] The ordinance creating the Committee and granting it almost dictatorial authority was not even presented until two days later.

John Randolph attended this Convention as delegate for the College, despite its constitutional irregularity. He was attacked for having supposedly accused Henry of being a "common robber" for compelling Corbin and Nelson to pay for the gunpowder. John Randolph was compelled to rise to deny that he had done so.[6]

The election on August 11 to fill Bland's seat on the Congressional delegation reveals, once again, the nearly equal division in the Convention, even after the new elections engineered by Randolph and the election of one-fourth of the delegates as new men. Frank Lee beat

Carter Braxton by a single vote. Lee was a radical. Braxton was the archetype of the James River conservatives. Affecting Lee's vote adversely would have been his brother's presence on the delegation; there would have been a natural hesitation to fill a seven-man delegation with two brothers of similar views. Braxton was a member of John Robinson's faction and was one of those most favored by his largesse, loans of public funds misdirected by Robinson to himself for that purpose. Braxton was still heavily in debt to the Robinson Estate. Lee's brother, Richard Henry Lee, was the primary leader who had exposed Robinson's misappropriation of public funds and caused financial difficulty or ruin to many of his supporters. Furthermore, Braxton had attempted to dissuade Henry from leading militia to Williamsburg to enforce payment for the gunpowder. When Henry demanded an endorser, or guarantor, for Receiver General Corbin's draft in payment for the gunpowder, Henry refused to accept Braxton's offer to endorse it. Henry had thereby publicly questioned Braxton's ability to pay or his intent to honor the draft if called upon to do so, implying Braxton's disloyalty to the common cause. Either of these interpretations amounted to publicly impugning Braxton's integrity and honor. Such an affront would last for a lifetime, and Braxton's friends would join him in hostility toward Henry. With knowledge of the two candidates' biographies, the Convention just barely favored Lee in a highly charged election. The weakness of Braxton's support is shown by the weak showing he made in the election for the Committee of Safety.

Randolph's Policy Triumphs and Pendleton Leads Virginia into Revolution

An even more important election was that for the Convention's executive, the Committee of Safety, on August 16, only five days later. Radical leaders were well represented: Mason, another Lee brother, Thomas Ludwell Lee, Page, and Digges. Notably, the conservatives were not only represented but had the Presidency of the Committee, Pendleton, along with Braxton and Mercer. The makeup of this Committee in a sense concluded Randolph's work and confirms his success. The most talented and prominent leader of the conservatives was

Pendleton. The radicals had triumphed. Their policies had invited war, and war and separation from Britain were obviously under way. Instead of their opponents' being driven out of office, or worse, they were brought into the leadership of the new regime, even in the face of bitter personal divisions. Up until this point, the conservative leaders, such as Pendleton and Harrison, might have pled before some future Court after Royal authority had been restored, that they had used their best efforts to effect reconciliation and encourage submission. Now that the break with Britain had come, these leaders knowingly put their own necks into the noose as surely as the radicals had already done. Both radicals and conservatives were united in the armed break from Britain from this point forward, however much they had differed to this point. The die was now cast—together—for all of them.

It was also on August 16, as if in recognition that Randolph's work had been accomplished, that the Convention unanimously recommended to Randolph that he should go home to rest for the next session of the Congress. Conservatives took the helm of the Convention upon Randolph's departure: Nicholas as President pro tem and Harrison as Chairman of the Committee of the Whole. Having stayed in the chair until this point, seeing that Virginia now had a new government and a new executive and that both sides were now irrevocably committed in unity to complete the work of freeing Virginia from the threat of British subjugation, Randolph went home. He had brought Virginia into the storm united.

The Second Continental Congress, September 6, 1775, and the Death of Peyton Randolph

Peyton and Betty Randolph left Williamsburg on August 27, 1775. They drove to Philadelphia and arrived in time for the September 6 session of the Second Continental Congress. They housed with Jefferson, Thomas Nelson, Jr., and some delegates from other colonies. The Congress was unable to assemble a quorum until September 13.[1]

John Hancock, elected President when Randolph resigned to return to Williamsburg for the June 1, 1775, General Assembly, did not resign as President upon Randolph's return. It is not clear whether Samuel and John Adams' understanding that he would do so was based on unclear or indefinite discussions between them and Hancock or whether Hancock violated an agreement or whether Randolph declined due to his health. When Hancock made no move to step aside, Randolph made no comment on his failure to do so.[2] It seems more likely that he recognized the precariousness of his health after the prolonged strains to which he had been subjected and quietly declined to take up the chair again. Otherwise, the sense of grievance over a breach, even of a gentleman's agreement, would have adversely affected the relations of the Virginians with the Massachusetts delegation. No such breach or ill feeling was apparent. The failure to appoint Randolph as chairman of a major committee points to the same conclusion: namely, that he intentionally declined responsibility for which his state of health was no longer suited.

The Congress's petition to the King had passed in July before the recess.[3] The King's answer was prompt. On August 23, 1775, he issued a Proclamation, augmenting Parliament's February declaration that Massachusetts was in a state of rebellion. The King promised decisive military action against a rebellion "manifestly carried on for the purpose of establishing an independent empire."[4] The King publicly recognized the radicals' goal of independence, which many colonists and their delegates were still unwilling to support. When the King's Proclamation of August 23 reached Philadelphia, the reconcilers were finally silenced. By mid–October 1775, all hope of reconciliation had vanished.[5]

Wren Building, exterior, College of William and Mary, Williamsburg (Colonial Williamsburg Foundation, No. T1991-1326).

On September 22, Randolph was appointed to the Committee on Trade, chaired by Benjamin Franklin. On October 2, it reported preliminary proposals to modify the Continental Associations in order to open the ports to importation from other nations of goods necessary for the war.[6] Work on those proposals were reported out of committee on November 1, 1775.

On Sunday, October 22, Peyton and Betty Randolph and Jefferson went to dinner at the country home of a Mr. Hills. After dinner, Randolph began to choke and then suffered a severe stroke. By 8:00 p.m. he was dead.[7]

Randolph was laid in state at the house where he and Betty boarded. On Tuesday, October 24, he received a state funeral at Christ

Wren Chapel, College of William and Mary, Williamsburg (Colonial Williamsburg Foundation, No. T1983-111).

22. Second Continental Congress, September 6, 1775

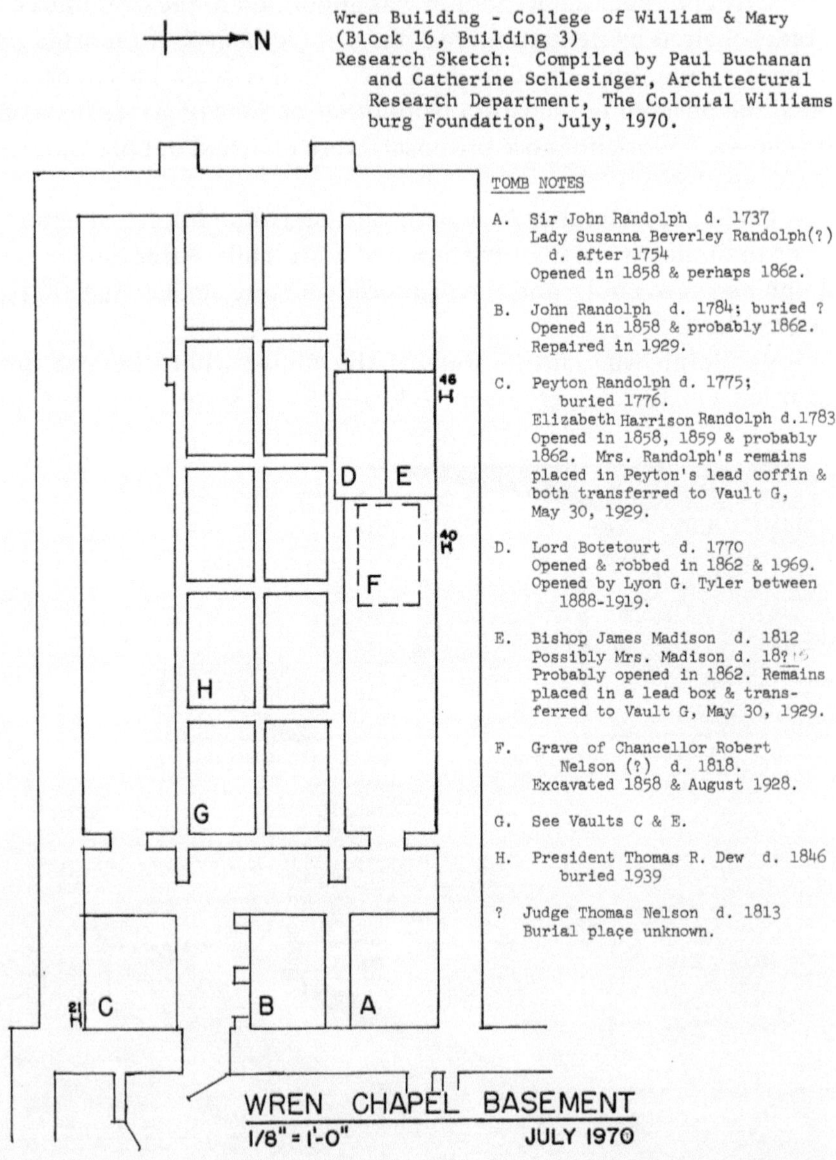

Wren Chapel Tomb Notes, 1970 research sketch compiled by Paul Buchanan and Catherine Schlesinger (Architectural Research Department, Colonial Williamsburg Foundation).

Church and was temporarily interred there. When news of his death reached Washington's headquarters, Edmund Randolph was given leave to travel to Philadelphia to escort Betty back to Williamsburg. In November 1776, Edmund returned to Philadelphia to escort Randolph's casket to Williamsburg. An honor guard met Edmund and the casket outside the town and escorted the casket to the family vault in the chapel of the College of William and Mary.[8]

Randolph's Will left almost all his estate to Betty for life, then to his brother John for life, and on his death to Edmund, who was instructed to give £500 to each of Edmund's sisters. The estate, valued at £12,980, included plantations in York, James City, and Charlotte Counties as well as the home in Williamsburg.

23

Summary

As I stated at the outset, the purpose of this work is to examine how it was that Virginia went into the Revolution united, when no other major colony did so. Its thesis is that Peyton Randolph foresaw the drift of Britain's policy as early as December 1768–April 1769 and its likely result, and that, as one of the great politicians of history, he made it his work to hold Virginia together as it entered the storm. No other colony, with the possible exceptions of Rhode Island, New Hampshire, Delaware, and Maryland, avoided a civil war as it pursued revolutionary severance from Britain. Among the larger colonies, only Virginia did so.

I have argued this in detail as Virginia moved, step by step, toward separation and war. I will not argue in such detail again, though I will give page references to prior arguments.

I do think it helpful to sum up the events which reveal Randolph's unexpressed intent, step by step. I submit that the purpose of this work has been satisfied and that the thesis of this work has been proven.

1753. The Pistole Fee Dispute. (See pages 19–22.) At considerable cost to himself at the time of his choice, Randolph accepted appointment as the House of Burgesses' agent and unequivocally chose his loyalty to Virginia and the Burgesses over his loyalty to the Crown and to England. He never thereafter wavered from that decision, even though his own family were painfully divided and close relatives chose exile.

1764–1765. The Stamp Act. (See pages 35–40.) Randolph was chairman of the committee in November and December 1764 that drafted the General Assembly's petitions regarding the Stamp Act. There is no doubt that he believed the Stamp Act to be unconstitutional. If Parliament has the right to tax the colonies, "the colonies are but the slaves of Britain." Those are harsh words, a view which Randolph held even before Richard Bland published his pamphlet in 1766, though some Burgesses conceded Parliament's right to do so. Randolph's confidence in the efficacy of persistent, reasonable petitions was not shaken by the Stamp Act controversy.

I am puzzled by the failure of other historians to avail themselves of the fruits of Bernard Knollenberg's work, showing that the policy of the British government was to restrict the colonies to the Eastern seaboard in order to enrich Britain and to maintain the colonies in due subservience to Britain. A large new Ireland.

March 1768. The Townshend Acts. (See pages 65–66.) Randolph, now the Speaker, appointed a small minority of radical rank and file to the committee drafting the petitions, again asserting that Parliament had no right to levy internal taxes in Virginia. He thereby tested their willingness to accept petition as the remedy, in order to achieve unity as to the unconstitutionality of the tax. Virginia did not join Massachusetts in a non-importation agreement. Bland's pamphlet had been published since the House had last confronted this issue, and this time the Burgesses were unanimous in denying Parliament's right to tax Virginia.

Between the March 1768 and May 1769 sessions of the House, the Ministry proposed the revival of treason statutes from the reign of Henry VIII, which would allow transportation of colonial leaders to England for trial. On October 1, 1768, British troops disembarked in Boston.

November 8, 1768. King George III's Speech from the Throne at the Opening of Parliament. (See pages 68–69.) The King declared Massachusetts to be in a state of disobedience and asked Parliament to punish its leaders. He specifically ordered his Governor to compile a list of those leaders likely guilty of treason within the last year so that he could appoint a special commission to hear and determine which accused persons should be transported to England for trial, reviving Henry VIII's treason statutes. Within the month, Parliament endorsed the King's proposal and revived three old treason statutes. The Governor and Attorney General of Massachusetts reviewed the recent proceedings of the Massachusetts legislature and other documents and eventually found no ground for an accusation of treason.

May 8, 1769. Randolph Amends the Speaker's Address to the Governor. (See pages 60–61.) On the opening day of a new General Assembly, Randolph, as Speaker, asserted that the House of Burgesses "lay claim to all its Ancient Rights and Privileges," instead of petitioning the Governor that the House "might enjoy all their Ancient Rights and Privileges." This claim was prelude to the Session.

May 16, 1769. The Secret Session of the House. (See pages 70–71.) On the opening day of the session, Randolph had had copies of three treason statutes of Henry VIII, revived by Parliament, laid on the table for examination by the members. Under these statutes, a defendant could be tried in England for treason committed anywhere. Going into secret session on May 16 in order to avoid premature dissolution, the House passed three resolutions without a dissenting voice: (1) The sole taxing authority was in the House of Burgesses. (2) The right to petition the King for redress of grievances included the right to request support from other colonies. (3) Trial for any crime committed in Virginia must be held in Virginia. These three resolutions confronted head-on the King, Ministry, and Parliament. A fourth resolution called for an Address to the King, which was likewise approved without dissent. Randolph appointed three radicals, including Henry and Lee, to a six-man committee to draft the petition to the King.

May 16–19, 1769. Agreement of Association and Radicals Brought into the "Government." (See pages 71–73.) Ninety-nine out of 116 Burgesses signed the Articles agreeing to non-importation of the taxed articles and many other specified types of British goods. Randolph appointed Washington, Henry, and Lee to the drafting committee. This General Assembly and the meeting of Associators were the first time that the radical leaders had been brought into the leadership group, or "government."

November 1768–April 1769. Timing and Cause of Randolph's Change of Course. (See pages 66–69.) Randolph knew of the Ministry's proposal of transportation for trial and the arrival of troops in Boston. The principle changes in circumstances between the March 1768 and May 1769 sessions were the King's Speech, including his announcement of his intent to inquire into the conduct of Massachusetts' radical leaders with transportation as the object, and Parliament's approval of transportation for trial. These events placed all colonial leaders at great risk, personally, if they opposed Britain's efforts to tax the colonies and its unfolding policy of subjugation. There was no expectation of a change in London's position in the near future. It was a newly elected Parliament under absolute Tory control and a King and Ministry asserting their willingness to use force both in Britain and in the colonies. There was no safety for himself or Virginia without some form of autonomy from Britain. It is clear that it was the threat of trial in Britain for treason and the inquiry in Massachusetts against the leaders of that colony, posing a fatal threat to the leaders of every other colony, that caused Randolph's change of course. The policy resulting from that change was well planned before the House convened in May 1769.

March 12, 1773. The New Committee of Correspondence. (See pages 91–96.) In June 1772, a Customs cutter, the *Gaspee*, had been burned by a Rhode Island mob. The Ministry authorized a Court of Inquiry with power to arrest defendants for trial for treason in England. Unlike the 1768–1769 investigation in Massachusetts, which made an investigation to determine whether treason had occurred and then found no evidence of treason, the action of burning the *Gaspee* had already been determined in London to have been treasonable. The Commission was appointed to find the participants in the mob and then to turn them over to a naval officer for transportation. Transportation for trial was to be put into effect for the first time. This followed 1770 incidents in London, in which the Lord Mayor of London had been sent to the Tower for resisting Parliamentary encroachment on the rights of the City of London, and in Massachusetts, in which troops had fired on a mob.

At the session of the Burgesses following the *Gaspee* incident, on March 12, 1773, the radical leaders proposed (1) a new Committee of Correspondence, independent of the Council, to maintain communications with other colonies and with its own agent in London, and (2) that the new Committee inform themselves of the *Gaspee* incident and the Court of Inquiry. Both resolutions passed without opposition.

23. Summary

The makeup of the new Committee reveals Randolph's consultation with the radicals, because his procedural genius had fashioned a powerful weapon against Britain. This was Randolph's invention. Neither the U.S. Congress nor any State legislature of which I am aware has ever had such a standing committee, which contained the entire leadership of that legislative body. The Committee included the Speaker, the chairmen of the six standing committees of the House, and four Members appointed by the Speaker. Lee was the only radical chairman of a standing committee. Randolph balanced the committee by prior agreement with the radicals, so that the committee was equally divided, and he had the controlling vote. The same was true of a Select Committee of three members who could act when the full Committee were unavailable, likewise one radical, one conservative, and Randolph.

A Governor could no longer deprive Virginia of leadership by refusing to convene the Burgesses, as occurred during the Stamp Act controversy. The inclusion of all the chairmen and the radical leaders assured that any action approved by the Committee would be approved by the House.

As the Ministry, backed by the King and Parliament, moved to put transportation into effect, Randolph's action shows that he had concluded that a break of some sort with Britain was both likely and necessary. As other colonies followed Virginia's lead, suppression of legislatures would not break communication between them. This was the first step toward a revolutionary organization among the colonies that would not follow radical Massachusetts but would, and did, follow Virginia's lead.

May 16–30, 1774. Response to the Boston Port Act. (See pages 102–110.) Outrage in the Burgesses was so high when they received news of the Boston Port Act about May 16, 1774, that the radicals had the votes to "do something," even though no news had been received as to Boston's response. The Day of Fasting and Prayer was approved without dissent, but it triggered a dissolution and delayed Virginia's response by two months.

After the Governor's dissolution of the House, a new Association was organized, following the 1769 precedent. Without news from Boston, its non-importation agreement was limited in scope. As Moderator of the Association, Randolph could call for the August Convention. Even before the August Convention, many county committees of Associator began to function. The August Convention broadened and simplified the scope of non-importation and created the county committees to enforce it. It also was able to elect delegates to the First Continental Congress. The Committee of Correspondence was able to act, even though the Governor had dissolved the House. Randolph's construction of such a centralized committee of the House proved its value. Unlike the Stamp Act Congress, which Virginia could not attend because the Governor would not convene the General Assembly, Virginia could attend the First Continental Congress, and its leadership there was crucial. Without action by the Assembly or even the House of Burgesses, Virginia had created the county committees of Associators, which were in being and functioning when the Congress met. The county committees legitimized by the Congress, which became the new governments in time, were created on Virginia's model.

August 1, 1774. First Convention of the Association, Williamsburg. (See pages 111–115.) The radicals pushed a vote to halt all exports in 1774. They did not "slacken their pace," per Jefferson. They pushed farther than the Convention was willing to go, in opposition to Randolph, and they lost. The Convention voted to stop all imports but medicine, effective November 1,1774, and authorized creation of independent county militias, not subject to the Governor. The Convention elected a balanced delegation to the Congress, three radicals, three conservatives, and Randolph as chairman. Randolph had Jefferson's *Summary,* the most radical argument yet made, proposed by Jefferson as instructions to the delegates, read out loud in his home to the elected delegates and other members. These actions are consistent with the argument that Randolph foresaw war at least as early as March 1773.

September 5–October 23, 1774. First Continental Congress. (See pages 120–135.) Randolph initially helped engineer his election as President and an end run around the hostile Pennsylvania delegation to place a Pennsylvania radical in the Secretary's chair. As President, he created rules of procedure from many disparate traditions. He soon knew all the delegates better than any man there. Over the course of the first three or four weeks at dinners and visits, he described how

23. Summary

Virginia had legitimized the local committees and how it had adopted a stricter, simplified non-importation rule—after bad results with complicated rules in 1769.

The Congress were closely divided between radicals and reconcilers. In mid–September, they unanimously responded to the Suffolk Resolves with an ambiguous resolution. While the Congress would endorse military training, it would not approve Lee's motion that the militias be well-supplied with arms and ammunition. Again, the radicals did not "slacken their pace." They got too far in front and did not have the votes. Lee did not even carry the Virginia vote, which means that Randolph voted against him in the Virginia caucus in order to avoid a vote that would deepen the opposition of the less ardent reconcilers. Randolph had a better feel for what the delegates would do. The critical vote was on Galloway's resolution, which would have trivialized the Congress, and was tabled by a vote of 6–5. With twelve delegations voting (Georgia did not attend), one delegation caucus was tied and did not cast its colony's vote; a change of one vote in that delegation, or likely in some other delegations, would have lost the motion to table. Randolph counted the votes and timed the decision on the motion to table when he had the votes to do so. A razor-thin victory. Only at the end of the Congress, on October 22, were there votes to kill it altogether.

The Congress approved a non-importation rule like Virginia's and delayed an embargo on exports, as Virginia desired. The Congress authorized local committees on Virginia's model to enforce the embargo, which became the new interim governments as constitutional structures dissolved under Royal opposition. Again, Randolph's procedural ability, which foresaw the uses to which the local committees and their Colony-wide Conventions could be put, laid the foundation for revolution. The legitimization of the committees was more valuable than the non-importation agreement, which failed to accomplish its purpose of creating pressure in Britain to force Parliament to change course.

Finally, the small-scale war between Virginia and Pennsylvania, stirred up by Governor Dunmore, never even surfaced during the Congress. One cannot prove how it was that "the dog did not bark," but it seems probable that Randolph had a hand in defusing the issue.

176

As local committees involving 7,000 members were organized throughout the colonies that fall and winter of 1774–1775, the King and Parliament drew a harder line. In the King's Speech from the Throne on November 29, 1774, King George III declared that he would resist all efforts to impair the authority of Parliament over all dominions of the Crown. In February, Parliament formally declared Massachusetts to be in rebellion and asked the King to enforce obedience to Parliament.

March 29, 1775. Virginia's Second Convention, Richmond. (See pages 140–146.) It differed from the First Convention in August 1774, whose delegates were all members of the old and the new Burgesses. Randolph, doubtlessly after having consulted the new standing super-committee, had called for new elections for the Second Convention. The delegates were elected by the new local committees, a more radical constituency than the voters in a county election, as Randolph clearly intended. One-fourth of the delegates had never served in the Burgesses.

Unlike the August 1774 Convention, Randolph opened this Convention with the formalities of the House of Burgesses and had the rules of the House adopted as the rules of the Convention. He intended the Convention to act on the very borderline of constituting itself as the government of Virginia. Randolph put all delegates on notice: "We are to be treated as rebels." The noose—or even being hanged, drawn, and quartered—threatened every delegate.

Henry and Lee presented a resolution to embody, arm, and discipline a militia, independent of the Governor, with provisions for financing it. Three of the delegates to the Congress—Pendleton, Harrison, and Bland—and the Treasurer, Nicholas, chairmen of four of the six standing committees of the House, all spoke against the proposal. Patrick Henry declaimed that there was no longer any peace, and his conclusion, "Give me liberty, or give me death!" was not a mere oratorical flourish. He would be a leading candidate for a treason trial. The resolution carried by five votes; a switch of three delegates in a Convention of 107 or more would have defeated it. Undoubtedly, it was Randolph who counted the votes and advised on the contents and timing of the resolution. Had it failed, three weeks before Lexington and Concord, Virginia would have gone into the Revolution with no plan for a military force. With Randolph in the chair, all had their say, and no one felt run over. Randolph appointed the leading conservatives—Pendleton, Harrison, and Nicholas—to the committee to prepare to put Virginia in a state of defense. All the delegates closed ranks and approved the committee's plan unanimously. What an amazing accomplishment! And some historians say that Randolph was too cautious! How much closer to the edge of one's support can you get?

May 10–24, 1775. The Second Continental Congress. (See pages 154–156.) During the two weeks that Randolph was again in the chair, the main issue was whether the reconcilers would block preparation for the war that had already begun. Pendleton, with Dickinson of Pennsylvania, was a leading proponent of reconciliation, even at this late date. On May 21 Pendleton instead became the advocate of compromise, to pursue both preparation for war and a final attempt at reconciliation simultaneously. The hand of Randolph can be seen in this change of position. While Pendleton could speak in the Congress as he wished, he could vote only in his delegation's caucus. Randolph probably assured him that he would not carry Virginia's vote. Pendleton's presentation of the reconciler's argument and his later switch to compromise gave the reconcilers assurance that they had been heard and would be given one more try to appease Britain. This was necessary to convince many that no choice was available other than submission or revolution and war, both of them dreadful alternatives. It is clear that Randolph did not think that reconciliation was possible, but it was important to carry the reconcilers along with the war party. That is what Randolph and Pendleton accomplished. Though the final vote for compromise took place after Randolph left for Williamsburg, the decision had already been reached. Bland's departure along with Randolph reduced the Virginia delegation to five, controlled by Henry, Lee, and Washington. I find it likely that Randolph suggested that Bland accompany him and Betty, in view of Bland's declining health and their having a common destination, Williamsburg. Perhaps Bland's departure along with Randolph was a condition of the agreement with Pendleton, so that, if it came to that, the radicals would continue to control the delegation. Bland's departure assured that Virginia's delegation would not be deadlocked.

July 17, 1775. The Third Convention, Richmond. (See pages 161–164.) The election of delegates to the Congress continued a balanced delegation with Randolph as the controlling vote: radicals Lee, Jefferson, and Nelson and conservatives Harrison, Bland, and Wythe. When Bland declined his reelection, Frank Lee was elected over Carter Braxton by only one vote. While other factors were also in play, the closeness of the vote again shows the even division of the Convention. Frank Lee's victory was important as assuring radical control of the delegation in view of Randolph's obviously declining health.

The critical decision was the election of a strong executive, the Committee of Safety, with a conservative, Pendleton, at its head, joined by Braxton and Mercer. In their very moment of triumph, the radicals accepted the conservatives and the elevation of their leader as the head of the Revolution in Virginia. And the conservatives cast away any possibility of amnesty by vigorously thrusting their own heads into the noose with the radicals. While many differences of personalities and policies would continue to affect Virginia's politics, all were united in Revolution and war against Britain. This was Randolph's great achievement.

The list of Tory leaders who left Virginia or committed suicide totaled five in number. These names were not illustrative; rather, they call the entire roll of prominent Virginia Tories. To be sure, there were foreigners living in Virginia who were Tories, primarily Scottish merchants representing firms in Glasgow, or even some English merchants. But these people were not Virginians, any more than Englishmen in later years who went out to India became Indians. The final proof of Randolph's success is the list of native-born Virginians who filed claims under the Treaty of Paris—a total of between thirteen and twenty-four. The scores of thousands who left, or were driven out, of other colonies underscore the difference between the unity of the Virginians and the civil wars waged in the rest of the colonies. Better leadership made the difference, and the leader was one of history's most successful politicians, Peyton Randolph.

Appendix
Early Randolph Family History

Sir John Randolph was the fifth of seven sons, along with two daughters, of William Randolph of Turkey Island and Mary Isham Randolph. William had settled on a peninsula in the James River in Henrico County (Richmond) known as "Turkey Island." His father, Richard Randolph, died in Dublin in 1671, and his mother, Elizabeth Ryland Randolph, died two years later. He was "sponsored" in Virginia by his uncle, Henry Randolph. Wilton House was built at Turkey Island by William Randolph III, the son of Sir John's brother, William II, the first cousin of Peyton Randolph. Wilton House was moved to a site above the Falls many years later to save it from industrial encroachment.

As we will see, Henry Randolph came to Virginia as a protégé of Governor Sir William Berkeley in 1642. He was advanced by that connection and reciprocated loyally through Sir William's ups and downs. In his later years, he sponsored his nephew, William Randolph of Turkey Island, who thereby benefitted from the continued favor of Governor Berkeley upon his arrival in Virginia. After the deaths of both Henry Randolph and Governor Berkeley, a close family connection between William Randolph of Turkey Island and his first cousin, Henry's son, Henry Randolph II, continued to benefit each.

The grandfather of William Randolph of Turkey Island was William Randolph, Gentleman, of Little Houghton Parish, Northamptonshire. He married twice, having three sons and a daughter by his first marriage and four sons and three daughters by his second wife, Dorothy Lane. The second son of the latter marriage was Richard Randolph of Morton Morrall (also called Morton Hall and Morton Morrell). Richard's oldest son, also named Richard, became a member of the Livery Company of Stationers, an honorable and expensive position in the City of London. Richard's second son was William Randolph, who emigrated to Virginia, settling at Turkey Island. The third son of William Randolph, Gentleman, by Dorothy Lane was Henry Randolph. A fourth son, Thomas, died in service with Prince Rupert nine days before the battle of Naseby in June 1645, which sank the King's cause.

Dorothy Lane Randolph's brother was Richard Lane. He is important to this narrative due to his prominence as a lawyer, from whose kinship his nephew, Henry Randolph, and his great-nephew, William Randolph of Turkey Island, both benefitted. Lane became close to the Court of King Charles I. He was appointed Attorney General to the Prince of Wales in 1634. Lane was prominent at the Middle Temple, one of the Four Inns of Court in London that served the legal profession and educated young men, beginning at the age of 14 or 15, some for the law and some just to acquire polish and range of acquaintance with the gentry from all over England. Lane published the first collection of reports of the Court of Exchequer, establishing a reputation for scholarship. In 1629 he was a "Reader," who gave one of the two annual series of lectures to instruct students, and also lawyers, in the law. His shield was mounted in the Middle Temple Hall. In the early 1630's he became a "Bencher," the board which governed the Middle Temple.

In 1637 he was Treasurer of the Middle Temple, the chairman of the Benchers. His prominence resulted in his being selected as leader of the team of four lawyers who defended Thomas Wentworth, Earl of Strafford, the King's most important advisor, in Strafford's famous trial by impeachment for treason at Westminster, opening on March 22, 1641. Strafford's defense was so successful that the King's enemies abandoned their prosecution of the treason trial on April 10, 1641, and that same afternoon filed a bill of attainder instead. He was pronounced guilty of treason and condemned by Act of Parliament on April 26. Strafford was executed in an act of legal murder on May 12, 1641. Lane moved to Oxford with the Court during the Civil War. At Oxford, he was knighted and appointed Lord Keeper of the Seal by King Charles I. Sir Richard Lane went into exile and died impoverished before the restoration of Charles II in 1660.

Sir William Berkeley was a younger son of a younger line of an ancient family whose seat was Berkeley Castle on the Severn River. His family connections brought him an appointment in 1632 as gentleman of the privy chamber extraordinary, a position which gave him access to King Charles I on a regular basis. The King knighted him for his services in the First Bishops' War with Scotland in 1639. He did not achieve distinction in the Second Bishops' War with Scotland in late 1639 and 1640. With the execution of Strafford on May 12, 1641, he was ready to seek a change. With the help of friends and connections, he received his appointment as Governor and Captain-General of Virginia on July 31, 1641, only ten weeks after Strafford's execution. It took months for Berkeley to prepare to embark for Virginia. His appointment was public knowledge, and he encouraged from the outset the emigration to Virginia of men and families that would help build a Royalist colony. He sailed from England in November 1641, arrived in Virginia in January 1642 and was installed as Governor on March 8, 1642.[1] King Charles I raised the Royal Standard at Nottingham on August 22, 1642. He thereby summoned the feudal levies and all loyal subjects to rally to him, and the civil war had officially begun.

William and Dorothy Randolph must have surveyed their own, and the families,' possibilities with a fresh look after the Strafford trial and execution on May 12, 1641. All living sons twenty years of age and older appeared to be established; some of them may have made friends who would help the families survive the coming war. The sixth son, Henry, had been educated but was single and of military age, eighteen. In 1637 or 1638, Henry undoubtedly took the benefit of his uncle's prominence at the Middle Temple to commence his studies there. He must have also shown signs of vigor and ability. He was chosen as the families' emigrant to Virginia to remove him from the coming war.

We can be sure that Sir William Berkeley and Richard Lane knew each other and saw each other at Court with some frequency, especially during the bitter weeks of the Strafford trial and execution. It is also probable that Lane knew of his sister's desire that Henry go to Virginia and spoke to Sir William about it after his appointment as Governor. In all probability Henry was prepped by his Uncle Richard and introduced by him to Sir William in late summer or early fall 1641. We know that Henry emigrated to Virginia before the King raised his standard on August 22, 1642; if he had still been in England, his duty would have been to join the King. It is not only likely, but highly probable, that Sir William encouraged the nephew of Strafford's successful legal defender to emigrate to Virginia. Under the circumstances, it was natural and inevitable that Henry became a protege and loyal ally of Governor Berkeley.

Henry received an appointment by Governor Berkeley as Henrico County Clerk, probably in 1642 but no later than 1644. As we will see, minority was no bar to holding such an office. The Governor appointed County Clerks until 1658; after that date, they were elected by the county justices who made up the County Court. The records of Henry's appointment as County Clerk and his activities for the next ten years were destroyed in one of three fires: by Bacon's rebels, who burned Jamestown in 1676, by British troops who burned much of Richmond in 1781, and by the Richmond fire in April 1865. Henry was qualified in that time and place by his education, which probably included some legal education at the Middle Temple, making him more knowledgeable about the functions of County Clerk than most settlers. At his death, he had a library, large for the time, of about 200 books. The family enjoyed a high level of education, generally, lawyers, clerics and a poet-dramatist friend of Ben Jonson.[2]

When Governor Berkeley called out the militia to oppose a landing by the Parliamentary Commissioners and troops in 1652, as described in Richard Bland's pamphlet above, Henry Randolph was a Captain of militia and undoubtedly supported the Governor with his presence and Henrico County Militia.[3]

Henry Randolph was elected Clerk of the Burgesses in 1656. The Clerk was one of two paid positions in the Burgesses, the other being the Speaker. The Clerk not only kept the records, but also kept the calendar and drafted legislation. He served as the Speaker's right hand. Henry kept this position until he died in 1673. Since the Speaker usually served for a single session, Henry's continuity in office made him particularly valuable. He kept his position as Henrico County Clerk also for a period of years, but had surrendered it sometime before 1665.[4]

As the military government of Oliver Cromwell became shaky

under his son, Richard Cromwell, Sir William Berkeley was elected Governor by the Assembly in March 1660, three months before Charles II returned to England, in breach of the terms of the Articles of Surrender with the Parliamentary Commissioners in 1652.[5] New Burgess elections were held, but no one then knew that this Assembly would continue in office until March 1676. The first Royalist Speaker of this new House was Henry Soane, a friend and neighbor of Governor Berkeley.[6] Henry Randolph and Henry Soane's daughter, Judith, were married in December 1661. The wedding was held at the house of Col. Francis Moryson, a close friend of the Governor, as witnessed by Moryson's service as Governor pro tem while Berkeley went to England to appear at Court in 1661–1662.[7]

Henry Randolph flourished under the new Royalist regime, receiving grants of various types from both the Governor and the Assembly. He acquired more property. About 1663 he built the first grist mill in Virginia at the Falls of Swift Creek near Petersburg, a structure recently renovated as a restaurant and theater.[8]

In either 1666 or 1669, Henry Randolph returned to England. By that time, his brother Richard and Richard's wife Elizabeth had moved to Dublin. Their second son, William Randolph, had been born in 1650. I consider it most likely that Henry's trip was in 1669, when William was nineteen. William's great-uncle, Sir Richard Lane, was well-remembered at the Middle Temple. After the Restoration, his memory was honored by a stained-glass window in Middle Temple Hall bearing his full coat of arms. In all probability, William was sent to the Middle Temple due to the continuing connection with it. William Randolph of Turkey Island later represented Henry's widow, Judith, as her attorney about 1678 in giving a bond to protect her son prior to her re-marriage.[9] William also became Attorney-General by 1698. He necessarily had read law, probably from 1664 or 1665 until 1669 at the Middle Temple. If so, William was in London when his uncle, Henry, arrived in 1669. Whether Henry went to Dublin to see Richard, or Richard came to London to see Henry, or neither, Henry and William would have seen each other in London in 1669 and had many opportunities to discuss Virginia.

William Randolph emigrated to Virginia in 1669 or soon after. He acquired property at Turkey Island, a bend in the James River about five miles from Henry's home on Swift Creek. Being south of the river, it was part of Henrico County until 1749, when Chesterfield County was created out of the portion of Henrico County lying south of the river. Because of the destruction of records, we do not know the manner in which William acquired this property, but he was settled there before Henry died in 1673. William was elected County Clerk by the Henrico County Justices in 1673 and served in that position until 1683, an arrangement undoubtedly made by Henry before his death.[10]

In the aftermath of Bacon's Rebellion in 1676, many of the rebels lost their property. One such tract of 1,230 acres known as "Curles," was on the James River one bend up-river from William's Turkey Island property. It had been owned by Nathaniel Bacon himself and escheated to the Crown. Governor Berkeley appointed William to appraise the Curles tract, and William then bought it at the price which he had set on it, £150, a favorable price, but not a shocking one, being substantially more than what was paid for unsettled land on the frontier, five shillings for one hundred acres. While the patent was not issued until years later, after the purchase price had been fully paid to the colony, the actual transaction was completed before Governor Berkeley left in 1677 on his last trip to England.[11] Governor Berkeley undoubtedly did William such a major favor both in view of his long friendship with Henry Randolph but also to cement William's relationship with Berkeley. At this time, William had been in Virginia only about five years, but with this acquisition, William Randolph of Turkey Island was launched on his own career. When Governor Berkeley died in England in 1677, William's position had already been solidified.

After Henry Randolph's death in 1673, William helped protect the family, especially young Henry II. In 1679, at age fourteen, young Henry gave a deposition regarding the weight of wheat delivered by William Randolph to a buyer. Henry obviously was working for William in some capacity for some period of time, in order to be aware of such details regarding William's business.[12] In 1683 William was elected a Justice of Henrico County and gave up his position as County Clerk. At that time, Henry Randolph II, having turned eighteen, was elected by the Justices as County Clerk to succeed his first cousin, William Randolph of Turkey Island, with an annual salary of 864 pounds of tobacco.[13] William was elected a Burgess for Henrico County in 1684, a position he held until 1698, when he became Speaker. Along the way, sometime before 1693 William became a militia Captain. In 1688, undoubtedly with William's assistance, Henry Randolph II was elected clerk of an Assembly committee to examine election returns.[14] In 1699 William became Clerk of the Burgesses, a position which he held until 1702.

Henry Randolph II died in 1693, at twenty-eight years of age. He left a widow, Sarah Swann Randolph, and one child, Henry Randolph III, born in 1689. William Randolph of Turkey Island was surety for Sarah when the grist and saw mill tract was divided, and the court order for the division provided that the division had to be satisfactory to William, enabling him to protect Sarah and young Henry III.[15] Sarah re-married to Captain Giles Webb, and William stood as surety for him when he was appointed guardian for Henry III.[16] When William Randolph of Turkey Island made his Will shortly before he died in 1711, one of his witnesses was Henry Randolph III, by then twenty-four years old. Considering William's prominence by then and the numerous friends and neighbors he could have called on for such a service, his desire to have his benefactor-uncle's grandson serve him in such an intimate way, surely speaks volumes regarding the relationship.[17]

When Captain Giles Webb died in 1713, Sarah was appointed executrix. William Randolph II stood as her surety along with Henry Randolph III, his second cousin.[18] In 1713 the Henrico County Justices recommended Henry Randolph III and Thomas Randolph of Tuckahoe as Justices, and both were elected.[19] Henry III served until his appointment as Sheriff by the Governor in 1723.[20] Henry died in 1726, leaving a widow, Elizabeth Eppes Randolph, and five small children. I find no evidence of maintenance of a close family connection between the two lines after Henry III's death.

Chapter Notes

Preface

1. Bernhard Knollenberg, *Growth of the American Revolution: 1766–1775* (Indianapolis: Liberty Fund, 2003), 247–249.
2. Thad W. Tate, "The Coming of the Revolution in Virginia: Britain's Challenge to Virginia's Ruling Class, 1763–1776," *The William and Mary Quarterly* 19, no. 3, (July 1962), 342.
3. Clifford Dowdey, *The Golden Age: A Climate for Greatness, Virginia 1732–1775* (Boston: Little, Brown, 1970), 352; Knollenberg, xlii.
4. Charles S. Sydnor, *American Revolutionaries in the Making: Political Practices in Washington's Virginia* (New York: Free Press, 1962), 94–95.
5. William Edwin Hemphill, *George Wythe, The Colonial Briton* (Ph.D. dissertation, University of Virginia, 1937), 224; Sydnor, 94.

Chapter 1

1. Notes for most of this chapter are given where treated in the body of the work.
2. John J. Reardon, *Peyton Randolph, 1721–1775: One Who Presided* (Durham: Carolina Academic Press, 1982), 71.
3. Reardon, 51.
4. Reardon, 39.

Chapter 2

1. Clifford Dowdey, *The Virginia Dynasties: The Emergence of "King Carter" and the Golden Age* (Boston: Bonanza, 1969), 157.
2. John J. Reardon, *Peyton Randolph, 1721–1775: One Who Presided* (Durham: Carolina Academic Press, 1982), 6.
3. Reardon, 6, 16.
4. Reardon, 17.
5. Reardon, 16.

Chapter 3

1. J. Kent McGaughey, *Richard Henry Lee of Virginia: A Portrait of an American Revolutionary* (Lanham: Rowman & Littlefield, 2004), 33–35; Alfred P. James, *The Ohio Company: Its Inner History* (Pittsburgh: University of Pittsburgh Press, 1959), 7–8.
2. McGaughey, 33.
3. Clifford Dowdey, *The Golden Age: A Climate for Greatness, Virginia 1732–1775* (Boston: Little, Brown, 1970), 67–69; Bernhard Knollenberg, *Growth of the American Revolution: 1766–1775* (Indianapolis: Liberty Fund, 2003), xlii; McGaughey, 33–34; James, 7–11.
4. McGaughey, 37.
5. McGaughey, 37–40; Eric Hinderaker and Peter C. Mancall, *At the Edge of Empire: The Backcountry in British North America* (Baltimore: Johns Hopkins University Press, 2003), 65–66, 95–97.
6. James, 95–104; McGaughey, 38.
7. John J. Reardon, *Peyton Randolph, 1721–1775: One Who Presided* (Durham: Carolina Academic Press, 1982), 17.
8. McGaughey, 38.

9. McGaughey, 41.

10. McGaughey, 45–46; Hinderaker and Mancall, 110–112.

11. McGaughey, 46.

12. McGaughey, 73.

Chapter 4

1. Clifford Dowdey, *The Golden Age: A Climate for Greatness, Virginia 1732–1775* (Boston: Little, Brown, 1970), 96–98.

2. Dowdey, *The Golden Age,* 99–101.

3. Dowdey, *The Golden Age,* 101.

4. John J. Reardon, *Peyton Randolph, 1721–1775: One Who Presided* (Durham: Carolina Academic Press, 1982), 10–11.

5. Landon Carter, *The Diary of Col. Landon Carter of Sabine Hall, 1752–1777,* edited with an Introduction by Jack P. Greene (Charlottesville: Published for the Virginia Historical Society, University Press of Virginia, 1965), vol. 1, 114–115; Dowdey, *The Golden Age,* 113–114.

6. William Edwin Hemphill, *George Wythe, The Colonial Briton* (Ph. D. dissertation, University of Virginia, 1937), 174.

7. Hemphill, 172–173.

8. Hemphill, 249.

Chapter 5

1. D. S. Freeman, *George Washington, Volume III* (New York: Charles Scribner's Sons, 1951), 215.

2. Clifford Dowdey, *The Golden Age: A Climate for Greatness, Virginia 1732–1775* (Boston: Little, Brown, 1970), 137, 223–224; J. Kent McGaughey, *Richard Henry Lee of Virginia: A Portrait of an American Revolutionary* (Lanham: Rowman & Littlefield, 2004), 83.

3. Bernhard Knollenberg, *Origin of the American Revolution: 1759–1766* (New York: Collier Books, 1961), 97–100; J. Kent McGaughey, *Richard Henry Lee of Virginia: A Portrait of an American Revolutionary* (Lanham: Rowman & Littlefield, 2004), 75–76.

4. McGaughey, 76; Thad W. Tate, "The Coming of the Revolution in Virginia: Britain's Challenge to Virginia's Ruling Class, 1763–1776," *The William and Mary Quarterly* 19, no. 3 (July 1962), 338.

5. Freeman, 215, 235.

6. Freeman, 198.

7. McGaughey, 95.

8. McGaughey, 97.

9. McGaughey, 96.

10. Alfred P. James, *The Ohio Company: Its Inner History* (Pittsburgh: University of Pittsburgh Press, 1959), 151.

11. Knollenberg, *Origin,* 101.

12. Bernhard Knollenberg, *Growth of the American Revolution: 1766–1775* (Indianapolis: Liberty Fund, 2003), 20–21.

13. Tate, 334; McGaughey, 83.

14. Knollenberg, *Origin,* 131–136.

15. Knollenberg, *Origin,* 164.

16. Knollenberg, *Origin,* 164–166.

17. Knollenberg, *Origin,* 166–167.

18. McGaughey, 83.

Chapter 6

1. Henry Mayer, *A Son of Thunder* (New York: Grove Press, 1991), 86.

2. David John Mays, *Edmund Pendleton: 1721–1803, Volume I* (Cambridge: Harvard University Press, 1952), 170.

3. Landon Carter, *The Diary of Col. Landon Carter of Sabine Hall, 1752–1777,* edited with an Introduction by Jack P. Greene (Charlottesville: Published for the Virginia Historical Society, University Press of Virginia, 1965), vol. 1, 7.

4. William Edwin Hemphill, *George Wythe, The Colonial Briton* (Ph.D. dissertation, University of Virginia, 1937), 188.

5. Hemphill, 194; Mays, 157–158; Clifford Dowdey, *The Golden Age: A Climate for Greatness, Virginia 1732–1775* (Boston: Little, Brown, 1970), 235–236; John J. Reardon, *Peyton Randolph, 1721–1775: One Who Presided* (Durham: Carolina Academic Press, 1982), 19–20.

6. Bernhard Knollenberg, *Origin of the American Revolution: 1759–1766* (New York: Collier Books, 1961), 204–209; Mayer, 76–78; Mays, 159–160; D. S. Free-

man, *George Washington, Volume III* (New York: Charles Scribner's Sons, 1951), 131.

7. Knollenberg, *Origin*, 207–208.

8. Mayer, 75–80; Mays, 161.

9. Mayer, 78–79, 81–83; Mays, 161–162; Freeman, 130–135; Dowdey, *The Golden Age*, 248–253; Reardon, 21–22.

10. Mayer, 83–87; Hemphill, 203; Mays, 161–162; Dowdey, *The Golden Age*, 253–254; Reardon, 22–23.

11. Mayer, 88–89, 91–93; Hemphill, 203; Mays, 163–164; Freeman, 137–139; Dowdey, *The Golden Age*, 255–258; Reardon, 22–23.

12. Bernhard Knollenberg, *Growth of the American Revolution: 1766–1775* (Indianapolis: Liberty Fund, 2003), 249.

13. Mark Puls, *Samuel Adams: Father of the American Revolution* (New York: Palgrave Macmillan, 2006), 49, 57; Reardon, 23–24.

14. Mayer, 94; Hemphill, 203.

15. Puls, 52–53; Mayer, 94–96.

16. Pauline Maier, *From Resistance to Revolution: Colonial Radicals and the Development of American Opposition to Britain, 1765–1776* (New York: W. W. Norton, 1991), 97; J. Kent McGaughey, *Richard Henry Lee of Virginia: A Portrait of an American Revolutionary* (Lanham: Rowman & Littlefield, 2004), 78; Dowdey, *The Golden Age*, 286–288.

17. McGaughey, 79–80; Dowdey, *The Golden Age*, 288; Mays, 171–172.

18. Dowdey, *The Golden Age*, 277–283; Reardon, 24.

19. Mayer, 96; Reardon, 25.

20. Mays, 169, 172.

21. Knollenberg, *Growth*, 7; Reardon, 25.

22. Mayer, 97; Knollenberg, *Growth*, 10–15.

23. Freeman, 164; Knollenberg, *Growth*, 1–15.

24. Maier, 145.

25. Mays, 170.

26. Mays, 157–158; Dowdey, *The Golden Age*, 235–236; Reardon, 19.

27. Richard Bland, *An Inquiry into the Rights of the British Colonies (ed. by E. G. Swem)* (Williamsburg, 1766; reprint: Richmond: Appeals Press, 1922), title page.

28. Bland, 23.

29. Bland, 24.

30. Edmund Randolph, *History of Virginia* (Charlottesville: Published for the Virginia Historical Society, University Press of Virginia, 1970), 149.

31. Randolph, 149–151; Warren M. Billings, *Sir William Berkeley and the Forging of Colonial Virginia* (Baton Rouge: Louisiana State University Press, 2004), 109–112; Bland, 24–26.

32. Bland, 26; Billings, 121–122, 127–129.

33. Bland, 28.

34. Bland, 29–30.

Chapter 7

1. J. Kent McGaughey, *Richard Henry Lee of Virginia: A Portrait of an American Revolutionary* (Lanham: Rowman & Littlefield, 2004), 82–83; David John Mays, *Edmund Pendleton: 1721–1803, Volume I* (Cambridge: Harvard University Press, 1952), 174–175.

2. Mays, 152–153, 174–177.

3. Henry Mayer, *A Son of Thunder* (New York: Grove Press, 1991), 104; Mays, 180; Clifford Dowdey, *The Golden Age: A Climate for Greatness, Virginia 1732–1775* (Boston: Little, Brown, 1970), 292.

4. Mayer, 106–107; John J. Reardon, *Peyton Randolph, 1721–1775: One Who Presided* (Durham: Carolina Academic Press, 1982), 26–27.

5. Mayer, 104–105; Reardon, 25–26; Mays, 181.

6. Mayer, 106–107, 113–114; McGaughey, 85.

7. Mayer, 112.

8. Mayer, 105, 112–113; Mays, 186–187.

9. Mays, 181–184; Reardon, 26.

10. Reardon, 29.

Chapter 8

1. John J. Reardon, *Peyton Randolph, 1721–1775: One Who Presided* (Durham: Carolina Academic Press, 1982), 32.

2. Reardon, 32; David John Mays, *Edmund Pendleton: 1721–1803, Volume I* (Cambridge: Harvard University Press, 1952), 252.

3. Reardon, 30.

4. Mark Puls, *Samuel Adams: Father of the American Revolution* (New York: Palgrave Macmillan, 2006), 70; D. S. Freeman, *George Washington, Volume III* (New York: Charles Scribner's Sons, 1951), 194–195; Bernhard Knollenberg, *Growth of the American Revolution: 1766–1775* (Indianapolis: Liberty Fund, 2003), 32–35.

5. Henry Mayer, *A Son of Thunder* (New York: Grove Press, 1991), 131.

6. Puls, 35–38; Knollenberg, *Growth,* 44, 264–267.

7. J. Kent McGaughey, *Richard Henry Lee of Virginia: A Portrait of an American Revolutionary* (Lanham: Rowman & Littlefield, 2004), 89; Knollenberg, *Growth,* 41.

8. Knollenberg, *Growth,* 157.

9. Knollenberg, *Growth,* 48–52.

10. Reardon, 30; Freeman, 198.

11. Mays, 249; Reardon, 30–31.

12. Freeman, 197–200; Reardon, 30–31.

13. Mays, 249.

14. Knollenberg, *Growth,* 56–57; Puls, 80–83.

15. Puls, 87.

16. Mays, 249–251; Mayer, 134–135; Reardon, 30.

17. Pauline Maier, *From Resistance to Revolution: Colonial Radicals and the Development of American Opposition to Britain, 1765–1776* (New York: W. W. Norton, 1991), 174–175; Knollenberg, *Growth,* 71–72; Freeman, 332.

18. Mayer, 132.

19. Freeman, 211.

20. Maier, 169.

21. Maier, 169.

22. Maier, 170–171.

23. Reardon, 33–34; Freeman, 219–220; Mayer, 139–141.

24. Reardon, 33–34.

25. Mayer, 141–143; Freeman, 221–222; Reardon, 34–35.

26. Freeman, 222; Mays, 254.

27. Mayer, 143–144; Freeman, 223–224.

28. William Edwin Hemphill, *George Wythe, The Colonial Briton* (Ph.D. dissertation, University of Virginia, 1937), 246.

29. Reardon, 35.

30. Knollenberg, *Growth,* 60–61.

31. Knollenberg, *Growth,* 60–61.

32. McGaughey, 90.

33. Puls, 74; Knollenberg, *Growth,* 56.

34. Maier, 177.

35. Clifford Dowdey, *The Golden Age: A Climate for Greatness, Virginia 1732–1775* (Boston: Little, Brown, 1970), 184.

36. Reardon, 35.

37. Freeman, 249–250.

38. H. J. Eckenrode, *The Randolphs: The Story of a Virginia Family* (Indianapolis: Bobbs-Merrill, 1946), 56.

39. Reardon, 36.

40. Reardon, 36–37.

41. Mays, 248–249.

42. Freeman, 248–249.

43. Freeman, 250.

44. Freeman, 251.

45. Freeman, 274.

46. Dowdey, *The Golden Age,* 311.

47. Freeman, 339.

48. Reardon, 38.

Chapter 9

1. Clifford Dowdey, *The Golden Age: A Climate for Greatness, Virginia 1732–1775* (Boston: Little, Brown, 1970), 47.

2. Bernhard Knollenberg, *Origin of the American Revolution: 1759–1766* (New York: Collier Books, 1961), 161–162.

3. Dowdey, *The Golden Age,* 222.

4. Dowdey, *The Golden Age,* 222–223.

5. Dowdey, *The Golden Age,* 177.

6. J. Kent McGaughey, *Richard Henry Lee of Virginia: A Portrait of an American Revolutionary* (Lanham: Rowman & Littlefield, 2004), 71–72.

7. David John Mays, *Edmund Pendleton: 1721–1803, Volume I* (Cambridge: Harvard University Press, 1952), 269.

8. Henry Mayer, *A Son of Thunder*

(New York: Grove Press, 1991), 73–74; McGaughey, 89; Mays 259.

9. McGaughey, 90; Mays, 256.

10. Mays, 142–144, 259; John J. Reardon, *Peyton Randolph, 1721–1775: One Who Presided* (Durham: Carolina Academic Press, 1982), 37.

11. Mays, 260, 267, 269, 273; D. S. Freeman, *George Washington, Volume III* (New York: Charles Scribner's Sons, 1951), 273, 347.

12. McGaughey, 63.

13. McGaughey, 45–46.

14. McGaughey, 46, 95.

15. Mays, 146.

16. Knollenberg, *Origin*, 161–163.

17. Dowdey, *The Golden Age*, 332.

18. Freeman, 235–238.

19. Freeman, 239–240.

20. Freeman, 252.

21. Jeff Broadwater, *George Mason, Forgotten Founder* (Chapel Hill: University of North Carolina Press, 2006), 60.

22. McGaughey, 95–102.

23. McGaughey, 103.

24. McGaughey, 100–102.

25. Freeman, 283–285, 299–301, 305–306, 333–334.

26. Broadwater, 62.

27. Knollenberg, *Origin*, 101.

28. Alfred P. James, *The Ohio Company: Its Inner History* (Pittsburgh: University of Pittsburgh Press, 1959), 155.

29. James, 158.

30. Broadwater, 62; James, 157.

31. Thad W. Tate, The Coming of the Revolution in Virginia: Britain's Challenge to Virginia's Ruling Class, 1763–1776," *The William and Mary Quarterly* 19, no. 3, (July 1962), 338.

32. Mayer, 149; Mark Puls, *Samuel Adams: Father of the American Revolution* (New York: Palgrave Macmillan, 2006), 122.

33. Pauline Maier, *From Resistance to Revolution: Colonial Radicals and the Development of American Opposition to Britain, 1765–1776* (New York: W. W. Norton, 1991), 177.

34. Maier, 186–187.

35. Maier, 202.

36. Maier, 170, 206–208.

Chapter 10

1. Henry Mayer, *A Son of Thunder* (New York: Grove Press, 1991), 172; Bernhard Knollenberg, *Growth of the American Revolution: 1766–1775* (Indianapolis: Liberty Fund, 2003), 93–97.

2. Mayer, 174.

3. Mayer, 174–175.

4. John J. Reardon, *Peyton Randolph, 1721–1775: One Who Presided* (Durham: Carolina Academic Press, 1982), 39.

5. Clifford Dowdey, *The Golden Age: A Climate for Greatness, Virginia 1732–1775* (Boston: Little, Brown, 1970), 320.

6. Charles S. Sydnor, *American Revolutionaries in the Making: Political Practices in Washington's Virginia* (New York: Free Press, 1962), 94; D. S. Freeman, *George Washington, Volume III* (New York: Charles Scribner's Sons, 1951), 316.

7. Reardon, 39; David John Mays, *Edmund Pendleton: 1721–1803, Volume I* (Cambridge: Harvard University Press, 1952), 268.

8. Reardon, 42; Freeman, 339.

9. Mark Puls, *Samuel Adams: Father of the American Revolution* (New York: Palgrave Macmillan, 2006), 131; Knollenberg, *Growth*, 98.

Chapter 11

1. D. S. Freeman, *George Washington, Volume III* (New York: Charles Scribner's Sons, 1951), 339.

2. Freeman, 339; Mark Puls, *Samuel Adams: Father of the American Revolution* (New York: Palgrave Macmillan, 2006), 140.

3. Puls, 141; Bernhard Knollenberg, *Growth of the American Revolution: 1766–1775* (Indianapolis: Liberty Fund, 2003), 105–106.

4. Freeman, 339–340; John J. Reardon, *Peyton Randolph, 1721–1775: One Who Presided* (Durham: Carolina Academic Press, 1982), 42–43.

5. Puls, 141–142; Clifford Dowdey, *The Golden Age: A Climate for Greatness, Vir-*

ginia 1732–1775 (Boston: Little, Brown, 1970), 322.

6. Puls, 139–140.
7. Puls, 144.
8. Puls, 144–147.
9. Dowdey, *The Golden Age,* 323.

Chapter 12

1. John J. Reardon, *Peyton Randolph, 1721–1775: One Who Presided* (Durham: Carolina Academic Press, 1982), 43–44; Clifford Dowdey, *The Golden Age: A Climate for Greatness, Virginia 1732–1775* (Boston: Little, Brown, 1970), 322–323; D. S. Freeman, *George Washington, Volume III* (New York: Charles Scribner's Sons, 1951), 348–349; Bernhard Knollenberg, *Growth of the American Revolution: 1766–1775* (Indianapolis: Liberty Fund, 2003), 119–122, 148.

2. Mark Puls, *Samuel Adams: Father of the American Revolution* (New York: Palgrave Macmillan, 2006), 151.

3. Knollenberg, *Growth,* 136–138; Puls, 152.

4. Henry Mayer, *A Son of Thunder* (New York: Grove Press, 1991), 193–194; Freeman, 358–359.

5. J. Kent McGaughey, *Richard Henry Lee of Virginia: A Portrait of an American Revolutionary* (Lanham: Rowman & Littlefield, 2004), 108–109; Pauline Maier, *From Resistance to Revolution: Colonial Radicals and the Development of American Opposition to Britain, 1765–1776* (New York: W. W. Norton, 1991), 225, 238, 264; Knollenberg, *Growth,* 141–145.

6. Puls, 154; Knollenberg, *Growth,* 139.
7. Knollenberg, *Growth,* 146–147.

Chapter 13

1. D. S. Freeman, *George Washington, Volume III* (New York: Charles Scribner's Sons, 1951), 350.

2. Henry Mayer, *A Son of Thunder* (New York: Grove Press, 1991), 186.

3. J. Kent McGaughey, *Richard Henry Lee of Virginia: A Portrait of an American Revolutionary* (Lanham: Rowman & Littlefield, 2004), 105.

4. Freeman, 350–351; John J. Reardon, *Peyton Randolph, 1721–1775: One Who Presided* (Durham: Carolina Academic Press, 1982), 44; Mark Puls, *Samuel Adams: Father of the American Revolution* (New York: Palgrave Macmillan, 2006), 152.

5. Freeman, 354.

6. John J. Reardon, *Edmund Randolph: A Biography* (New York: Macmillan, 1974), 17; Mayer, 190–191; Freeman, 352–353; David John Mays, *Edmund Pendleton: 1721–1803, Volume I* (Cambridge: Harvard University Press, 1952), 270.

7. Reardon, *Peyton Randolph,* 45–46.

8. Mayer, 190–192; Freeman, 355–356; Reardon, *Peyton Randolph,* 45; Bernhard Knollenberg, *Growth of the American Revolution: 1766–1775* (Indianapolis: Liberty Fund, 2003), 148–149.

9. Mayer, 191–193; Freeman, 355–357; Mays, 271–272; Reardon, *Peyton Randolph,* 46.

10. Reardon, *Peyton Randolph,* 46.

11. Reardon, *Peyton Randolph,* 46; Freeman, 355.

Chapter 14

1. Henry Mayer, *A Son of Thunder* (New York: Grove Press, 1991), 193–198; D. S. Freeman, *George Washington, Volume III* (New York: Charles Scribner's Sons, 1951), 357–367.

2. William Edwin Hemphill, *George Wythe, The Colonial Briton* (Ph.D. dissertation, University of Virginia, 1937), 267.

3. Mayer, 198.
4. Mayer, 198.
5. Freeman, 367.

6. John J. Reardon, *Peyton Randolph, 1721–1775: One Who Presided* (Durham: Carolina Academic Press, 1982), 48; Mayer 199–204.

7. Mark Puls, *Samuel Adams: Father of the American Revolution* (New York: Palgrave Macmillan, 2006), 152.

8. Freeman, p. 368.

9. Jeff Broadwater, *George Mason, Forgotten Founder* (Chapel Hill: University of North Carolina Press, 2006), 68.

10. Reardon, *Peyton Randolph*, 48–49.

11. Freeman, 368–369; Reardon, *Peyton Randolph*, 48–49.

12. Mayer, 199–204; David John Mays, *Edmund Pendleton: 1721–1803, Volume I* (Cambridge: Harvard University Press, 1952), 275–277.

13. Clifford Dowdey, *The Golden Age: A Climate for Greatness, Virginia 1732–1775* (Boston: Little, Brown, 1970), 324 ff.

14. Eric Hinderaker and Peter C. Mancall, *At the Edge of Empire: The Backcountry in British North America* (Baltimore: Johns Hopkins University Press, 2003), 157.

15. Jack M. Sosin, *The Revolutionary Frontier, 1763–1783* (New York: Holt, Rinehart, and Winston, 1967), 58–60; Hinderaker and Mancall, 157–158; Mayer, 185.

16. Hinderaker and Mancall, 158; Sosin, 58–60.

17. Sosin, 60.

18. Edmund Randolph, *History of Virginia* (Charlottesville: Published for the Virginia Historical Society, University Press of Virginia, 1970), 200–202.

19. Landon Carter, *The Diary of Col. Landon Carter of Sabine Hall, 1752–1777*, edited with an Introduction by Jack P. Greene (Charlottesville: Published for the Virginia Historical Society, University Press of Virginia, 1965), vol. 2, 812.

20. Neal O. Hammon and Richard Taylor, *Virginia's Western War, 1775–1786* (Mechanicsburg: Stackpole Books, 2002), xxx–xxxiv; Hinderaker and Mancall, 157–160; Carter, vol. 2, 812.

21. Mayer, 185; Wikipedia, "Yohogania County, Virginia."

Chapter 15

1. Henry Mayer, *A Son of Thunder* (New York: Grove Press, 1991), 205–207; David John Mays, *Edmund Pendleton: 1721–1803, Volume I* (Cambridge: Harvard University Press, 1952), 279–283; Clifford Dowdey, *The Golden Age: A Climate for Greatness, Virginia 1732–1775* (Boston: Little, Brown, 1970), 333–334; John J. Reardon, *Peyton Randolph, 1721–1775: One Who Presided* (Durham: Carolina Academic Press, 1982), 50.

2. Mayer, 207–208; Mark Puls, *Samuel Adams: Father of the American Revolution* (New York: Palgrave Macmillan, 2006), 159; J. Kent McGaughey, *Richard Henry Lee of Virginia: A Portrait of an American Revolutionary* (Lanham: Rowman & Littlefield, 2004), 112–114.

3. Puls, 260; Reardon, *Peyton Randolph*, 50.

4. Reardon, *Peyton Randolph*, 50; Puls, 160.

5. Puls, 156; D. S. Freeman, *George Washington, Volume III* (New York: Charles Scribner's Sons, 1951), 379; Mayer, 208–210.

6. Puls, 158–160.

7. Freeman, 374, 376; Mayer, 210–217; Mays, 283–286.

8. Freeman, 379–380.

9. Mayer, 222–224; Pauline Maier, *From Resistance to Revolution: Colonial Radicals and the Development of American Opposition to Britain, 1765–1776* (New York: W. W. Norton, 1991), 244.

10. Puls, 162; Mayer, 222; Freeman, 380–381.

11. Reardon, *Peyton Randolph*, 52; Freeman, 382; Mayer, 222–223; Mays, 289–290.

12. Freeman, 383; Mays, 293–295.

13. Freeman, 388; Reardon, *Peyton Randolph*, 52; Mayer, 223–224.

14. Maier, 279.

15. Mays, 295.

16. Reardon, *Peyton Randolph*, 53.

17. Reardon, *Peyton Randolph*, 53.

18. Freeman, 388.

19. Freeman, 389.

20. Freeman, 389.

21. Freeman, 389.

22. Freeman, 387.

23. Maier, 278–279.

24. Mays, 299.

25. Reardon, *Peyton Randolph*, 52.
26. Alfred P. James, *The Ohio Company: Its Inner History* (Pittsburgh: University of Pittsburgh Press, 1959), 170–174.

Chapter 16

1. D. S. Freeman, *George Washington, Volume III* (New York: Charles Scribner's Sons, 1951), 394.
2. John J. Reardon, *Peyton Randolph, 1721–1775: One Who Presided* (Durham: Carolina Academic Press, 1982), 55.
3. Henry Mayer, *A Son of Thunder* (New York: Grove Press, 1991), 234–235.
4. Mayer, 235.
5. Freeman, 395.
6. Freeman, 395.
7. Mayer, 236.
8. Bernhard Knollenberg, *Growth of the American Revolution: 1766–1775* (Indianapolis: Liberty Fund, 2003), 213.
9. Mayer, 238.
10. Pauline Maier, *From Resistance to Revolution: Colonial Radicals and the Development of American Opposition to Britain, 1765–1776* (New York: W. W. Norton, 1991), 236.
11. Knollenberg, *Growth*, 206.
12. Maier, 237; Freeman, 400.
13. Clifford Dowdey, *The Golden Age: A Climate for Greatness, Virginia 1732–1775* (Boston: Little, Brown, 1970), 328.
14. Knollenberg, *Growth*, 209.
15. Freeman, 400; Knollenberg, *Growth*, 210.
16. Knollenberg, *Growth*, 209–210.
17. Maier, 236–237.
18. Maier, 240–241.

Chapter 17

1. Henry Mayer, *A Son of Thunder* (New York: Grove Press, 1991), 240; John J. Reardon, *Peyton Randolph, 1721–1775: One Who Presided* (Durham: Carolina Academic Press, 1982), 55.

2. D. S. Freeman, *George Washington, Volume III* (New York: Charles Scribner's Sons, 1951), 401.
3. Reardon, *Peyton Randolph*, 56; Freeman, 402.
4. Reardon, *Peyton Randolph*, 56.
5. Mayer, 243.
6. Freeman, 402; Mayer, 243.
7. Reardon, *Peyton Randolph*, 57; Freeman, 403; Mayer, 241.
8. Mayer, 244.
9. Freeman, 403–405; Mayer, 244–246.
10. Mayer, 247.
11. Mayer, 247.
12. Mayer, 247; Freeman, 405–406; Bernhard Knollenberg, *Growth of the American Revolution: 1766–1775* (Indianapolis: Liberty Fund, 2003), 215.
13. Mayer, 247–248.
14. Reardon, *Peyton Randolph*, 57; Mayer, 248.
15. Mayer, 248; David John Mays, *Edmund Pendleton: 1721–1803, Volume I* (Cambridge: Harvard University Press, 1952), vol. 2, 12.
16. Mayer, 248; Reardon, *Peyton Randolph*, 57–58.
17. Mayer, 241.

Chapter 18

1. D. S. Freeman, *George Washington, Volume III* (New York: Charles Scribner's Sons, 1951), 407–410.
2. John J. Reardon, *Peyton Randolph, 1721–1775: One Who Presided* (Durham: Carolina Academic Press, 1982), 58; Freeman, 411; Henry Mayer, *A Son of Thunder* (New York: Grove Press, 1991), 249.
3. Reardon, *Peyton Randolph*, 58–59; Freeman, 411–412; Mayer, 249–250.
4. Mayer, 250–251; Reardon, *Peyton Randolph*, 59–60.
5. Mayer, 250.
6. Reardon, *Peyton Randolph*, 60; Mayer, 251.
7. Freeman, 412–414.
8. Mayer, 251–254.
9. H. J. Eckenrode, *The Randolphs:*

The Story of a Virginia Family (Indianapolis: Bobbs-Merrill, 1946), 95–97.

10. Mayer, 255–257.

Chapter 19

1. Henry Mayer, *A Son of Thunder* (New York: Grove Press, 1991), 262.

2. Clifford Dowdey, *The Golden Age: A Climate for Greatness, Virginia 1732–1775* (Boston: Little, Brown, 1970), 348–349.

3. D. S. Freeman, *George Washington, Volume III* (New York: Charles Scribner's Sons, 1951), 420.

4. John J. Reardon, *Peyton Randolph, 1721–1775: One Who Presided* (Durham: Carolina Academic Press, 1982), 61.

5. Reardon, *Peyton Randolph*, 61.

6. Reardon, *Peyton Randolph*, 61.

7. Mayer, 263.

8. Reardon, *Peyton Randolph*, p. 61.

9. Mark Puls, *Samuel Adams: Father of the American Revolution* (New York: Palgrave Macmillan, 2006), 172; Reardon, *Peyton Randolph*, 67.

10. Mayer, 263–264.

11. Wikipedia, "Conciliatory Resolution"

12. Bernhard Knollenberg, *Growth of the American Revolution: 1766–1775* (Indianapolis: Liberty Fund, Inc., 2003), 208–209.

13. Mayer, 263–265; Freeman, 434–438.

Chapter 20

1. John J. Reardon, *Peyton Randolph, 1721–1775: One Who Presided* (Durham: Carolina Academic Press, 1982), 62.

2. Reardon, *Peyton Randolph*, 62.

3. Reardon, *Peyton Randolph*, 62; John J. Reardon, *Edmund Randolph: A Biography* (New York: Macmillan, 1974), 19.

4. Reardon, *Edmund Randolph*, 19; Reardon, *Peyton Randolph*, 62.

5. Reardon, *Peyton Randolph*, 62–63.

6. William Edwin Hemphill, *George Wythe, The Colonial Briton* (Ph.D. dissertation, University of Virginia, 1937), 223.

7. Reardon, *Edmund Randolph*, 22, 391–392.

8. Reardon, *Edmund Randolph*, 20–21.

9. Clifford Dowdey, *The Golden Age: A Climate for Greatness, Virginia 1732–1775* (Boston: Little, Brown, 1970), 342.

10. Thad W. Tate, "The Coming of the Revolution in Virginia: Britain's Challenge to Virginia's Ruling Class, 1763–1776," *The William and Mary Quarterly* 19, no. 3, July 1962), 342; Bernhard Knollenberg, *Growth of the American Revolution: 1766–1775* (Indianapolis: Liberty Fund, 2003), 248.

11. Christopher Moore, *The Loyalists: Revolution, Exile, Settlement* (Toronto: Macmillan of Canada, 1984), 54, 102–104, 112–114.

Chapter 21

1. John J. Reardon, *Peyton Randolph, 1721–1775: One Who Presided* (Durham: Carolina Academic Press, 1982), 63–64; Henry Mayer, *A Son of Thunder* (New York: Grove Press, 1991), 268–269.

2. Mayer, 269–270; Reardon, *Peyton Randolph*, 63–64; David John Mays, *Edmund Pendleton: 1721–1803, Volume 2* (Cambridge: Harvard University Press, 1952), 34–36.

3. William Edwin Hemphill, *George Wythe, The Colonial Briton* (Ph.D. dissertation, University of Virginia, 1937), 274; Mayer, 272.

4. Mays, vol. 2, 361; Mayer, 272.

5. Mayer, 272; Mays, vol 2, 35–36.

6. Mayer, 271.

Chapter 22

1. John J. Reardon, *Peyton Randolph, 1721–1775: One Who Presided* (Durham: Carolina Academic Press, 1982), 67.

2. Reardon, *Peyton Randolph*, 61, 67–68.

3. Henry Mayer, *A Son of Thunder* (New York: Grove Press, 1991), 266.

4. Reardon, *Peyton Randolph*, 68; Pauline Maier, *From Resistance to Revolution: Colonial Radicals and the Development of American Opposition to Britain, 1765–1776* (New York: W. W. Norton, 1991), 241.

5. Maier, 241.

6. Reardon, *Peyton Randolph*, 67–68.

7. Reardon, *Peyton Randolph*, 68.

8. Reardon, *Edmund Randolph*, 22–23; Reardon, *Peyton Randolph*, 68–69.

Appendix

1. Warren M. Billings, *Sir William Berkeley and the Forging of Colonial Virginia* (Baton Rouge: Louisiana State University Press, 2004), 27–38.

2. Wassell Randolph, *Henry Randolph I of Henrico County, 1623–1773* [sic] *Virginia and his Descendants* (Memphis: Dossitt Library, 1952), 34.

3. Randolph, *Henry Randolph I*, 29.

4. Billings, 92; Randolph, *Henry Randolph I*, 32.

5. Billings, 120–125.

6. Billings, 133–135.

7. Randolph, *Henry Randolph I*, 28, 31–32.

8. Randolph, *Henry Randolph I*, 32.

9. Randolph, *Henry Randolph I*, 39.

10. Randolph, *Henry Randolph I*, 36.

11. H. J. Eckenrode, *The Randolphs: The Story of a Virginia Family* (Indianapolis: Bobbs-Merrill, 1946), 37–39; Wikipedia, "William Randolph of Turkey Island, Virginia."

12. Randolph, *Henry Randolph I*, 39.

13. Randolph, *Henry Randolph I*, 42.

14. Randolph, *Henry Randolph I*, 42.

15. Randolph, *Henry Randolph I*, 44, 47.

16. Randolph, *Henry Randolph I*, 45.

17. Randolph, *Henry Randolph I*, 48.

18. Randolph, *Henry Randolph I*, 50.

19. Randolph, *Henry Randolph I*, 49.

20. Randolph, *Henry Randolph I*, 49.

Bibliography

Billings, Warren M. *Sir William Berkeley and the Forging of Colonial Virginia.* Baton Rouge: Louisiana State University Press, 2004.

Bland, Richard. *An Inquiry into the Rights of the British Colonies.* Edited by E.G. Swem. Williamsburg, 1766. Reprint: Richmond: Appeals Press, 1922.

Broadwater, Jeff. *George Mason, Forgotten Founder.* Chapel Hill: University of North Carolina Press, 2006.

Carter, Landon. *Diary of Col. Landon Carter of Sabine Hall, 1752–1778.* 2 vols. Edited with Introduction by Jack P. Greene. Charlottesville: Published for the Virginia Historical Society, University Press of Virginia, 1965.

Dowdey, Clifford. *The Golden Age: A Climate for Greatness, Virginia 1732–1775.* Boston: Little, Brown, 1970.

Dowdey, Clifford. *The Virginia Dynasties: The Emergence of "King Carter" and the Golden Age.* Boston: Bonanza, 1969.

Dunn, Walter S. *Choosing Sides on the Frontier in the American Revolution.* Westport: Praeger, 2007.

Eckenrode, H. J. *The Randolphs: The Story of a Virginia Family.* Indianapolis: Bobbs–Merrill, 1946.

Freeman, D. S. *George Washington, Volume III.* New York: Charles Scribner's Sons, 1951.

Hammon, Neal O., and Richard Taylor. *Virginia's Western War, 1775–1786.* Mechanicsburg: Stackpole Books, 2002.

Hemphill, William Edwin. *George Wythe, The Colonial Briton.* Ph.D. dissertation. University of Virginia, 1937.

Hinderaker, Eric, and Mancall, Peter C. *At the Edge of Empire: The Backcountry in British North America.* Baltimore and London: Johns Hopkins University Press, 2003.

James, Alfred P. *The Ohio Company: Its Inner History.* Pittsburgh: University of Pittsburgh Press, 1959.

Jefferson, Thomas. *The Writings of Thomas Jefferson.* Edited by Andrew A. Lipscomb, editor-in-chief, and Albert Ellery Bergh, managing editor, issued by the Thomas Jefferson Memorial Foundation, Vol. XVIII, Washington, D.C., 1905. Sketches of Distinguished Men, Peyton Randolph, pages 135–140.

Knollenberg, Bernhard. *Growth of the American Revolution: 1766–1775.* Indianapolis: Liberty Fund, 2003.

Knollenberg, Bernhard. *Origin of the American Revolution: 1759–1766.* New York: Collier Books, 1961.

Maier, Pauline. *From Resistance to Revolution: Colonial Radicals and the Development of American Opposition to Britain, 1765–1776.* New York: W.W. Norton, 1991.

Malone, Dumas. *Jefferson the Virginian.* Boston: Little, Brown, 1948.

Mayer, Henry. *A Son of Thunder.* New York: Grove Press, 1991.

Bibliography

Mays, David John. *Edmund Pendleton: 1721–1803.* 2 vols. Cambridge: Harvard University Press, 1952.

McGaughey, J. Kent. *Richard Henry Lee of Virginia: A Portrait of an American Revolutionary.* Lanham: Rowman & Littlefield, 2004.

Moore, Christopher. *The Loyalists: Revolution, Exile, Settlement.* Toronto: Macmillan of Canada, 1984.

Philbrick, Nathaniel. *Valiant Ambition: George Washington, Benedict Arnold, and the Fate of the American Revolution.* New York: Viking, 2016.

Puls, Mark. *Samuel Adams: Father of the American Revolution.* New York: Palgrave Macmillan, 2006.

Randolph, Edmund. *History of Virginia.* Charlottesville: For Virginia Historical Society, University Press of Virginia, 1970.

Randolph, Wassell. *Henry Randolph I of Henrico County, 1623–1773* [sic] *Virginia and His Descendants.* Memphis: Dossitt Library, 1952.

Reardon, John J. *Edmund Randolph: A Biography.* New York: Macmillan, 1974.

Reardon, John J. *Peyton Randolph, 1721–1775: One Who Presided.* Durham: Carolina Academic Press, 1982.

Saunders, Robert Miller. *The Public Career of Robert Carter Nicholas.* M.B.A. thesis. University of Richmond, 1962.

Sosin, Jack M. *The Revolutionary Frontier, 1763–1783.* New York: Holt, Rinehart, and Winston: 1967.

Sydnor, Charles S. *American Revolutionaries in the Making: Political Practices in Washington's Virginia.* New York: Free Press, 1962.

Tate, Thad W. "The Coming of the Revolution in Virginia: Britain's Challenge to Virginia's Ruling Class, 1763–1776." *The William and Mary Quarterly* 19, no. 3 (July 1962).

Wikipedia, "Conciliatory Resolution."

Wikipedia, "William Randolph of Turkey Island, Virginia."

Wikipedia, "Yohogania County, Virginia."

Index

Index

Index

www.ingramcontent.com/pod-product-compliance
Ingram Content Group UK Ltd.
Pitfield, Milton Keynes, MK11 3LW, UK
UKHW041355190726
13851UKWH00014B/115